# THE PSYCHOLOGY OF TOURNAMENT GOLF
### Playing Your Best When It Means The Most

by
David L. Cook, PhD

A GAME-DAY PRIMER FOR ASPIRING CHAMPIONS

Foreword by

Jim Hardy
*2007 National PGA Teacher of the Year*

## BONUS INSTRUCTION
Introducing the Utopia Pre-Set Swing and Face-On Putting
*"A Revolutionary Approach to Blending the Mental Game, the Swing, and Putting"*

www.psychologyoftournamentgolf.com

Copyright © 2014 David L. Cook, Ph.D.
All rights reserved. No part of this book may be used or reproduced in any manner whatsoever without the written permsission of the author.

Published by Sacred Journey Stories

ISBN 978-0-9742650-8-7

**Printed in the United States of America**
*First Printing, August 2014*

Cover Design by Jeff Jones

# CONTENTS

| | |
|---|---|
| Endorsements | 3 |
| Dedication | 8 |
| Acknowledgements | 9 |
| Foreword | 10 |
| Introduction: Why Utopia | 16 |
| Chapter 1: The Quest | 19 |
| Chapter 2: Twenty Minutes Before the Trophy Celebration | 25 |
| Chapter 3: Pre-Game | 31 |
| Chapter 4: Game Time | 35 |
| Chapter 5: Accountability to the Process | 57 |
| Chapter 6: The Three-Challenge Process | 61 |
| Chapter 7: Fake It 'til You Make It | 67 |
| Chapter 8: Course Management | 69 |
| Chapter 9: Fun | 73 |
| Chapter 10: Post Round Game Day | 77 |
| Chapter 11: Conclusion | 81 |
| | |
| Bonus Section I: The Utopia Pre-Set | |
| Chapter 1: Finding the Slot | 85 |
| Chapter 2: Re-Ordering the Swing Components | 91 |
| Chapter 3: The Pre-Set Secret | 95 |
| Chapter 4: Conclusion | 103 |

Bonus Section II: Face-On Putting
Chapter 1: Truth vs. Tradition — 105
Chapter 2: The Putting Transformation — 109
Chapter 3: The Face-On Revelation — 111
Chapter 4: Face-On Putting Unveiled — 115
Chapter 5: Conclusion — 119

Wrap Up — 123

Epilogue — 125

About the Author — 128

Greatest Shots Journal — 132

Mental Toughness Journal — 133

# ENDORSEMENTS

"This is a masterpiece text on the final frontier: the mental game. Dr. Cook gives his best stuff in *The Psychology of Tournament Golf*. I wish I would have had this book at my finger tips when I played the PGA Tour. Any level competitor can benefit from the mental game wisdom of David Cook."

*Bill Rogers, 1981 British Open Champion and PGA Tour Player of the Year*

"I always believed there was a way to better bridge the technical and mental. In reading this book you will learn that it is not only possible, but also how to do it. David has developed some groundbreaking thoughts on making this happen. You are about to discover the bridge."

*Jim Hardy, 2007 National PGA Teacher of the Year, Best-Selling Author, Top 10 Golf Instructor—Golf Digest.*

*David L. Cook*

"David Cook has taken the abstract art of sports psychology and quantified it in the *Psychology of Tournament Golf*. Before I met David, I did not have a way to improve my mental game. His process and thoughts have given me a clear path to work on my mental game, to track it, and be able to identify and analyze tendencies. SFT"

*Billy Hurley III, PGA Tour*

"I love the game of golf. The Psychology of Tournament Golf provides game day mental game tactics that will serve you well. I can vouch for their effectiveness. These principles are the same strategies Dr. Cook and I used during my NBA career."

*David Robinson, NBA MVP 1995, NBA World Champion 1999, 2003, NBA Hall of Fame*

"*The Psychology of Tournament Golf* will help you play your best golf. I'm confident it will help you have more fun and shoot lower scores."

*Scott Simpson, U.S. Open Champion, 1987*

"*The Psychology of Tournament Golf* gives all competitors a common sense approach to the mental game. Dr. Cook's game day roadmap provides a fun and easy way for reaching your golfing dreams."

*Fred Funk, multiple PGA Tour winner*

"Dr. Cook reveals in this book the essential parts and processes you 'must have' to win at the highest level of competitive golf!"

*Tom Pernice, multiple PGA Tour winner*

"The golf course and tournament golf in particular is riddled with opportunities to get hit in the face with adversity. How you prepare mentally for a tournament, a round within the tournament and a shot within the round is the single most important differentiator between success and getting hit in the face. In this book, David lays out the groundwork to prepare mentally for success, to sign the masterpiece of the tournament, but also how to reset your goals to win tournaments within a tournament. This book is fabulous for a tournament golfer but also important for those who want to prepare to succeed at life."

*Joe Ogilvie, PGA Tour winner*

*David L. Cook*

"In golf, business and life success is about doing your best when it counts the most. David Cook outlines, in a simple consistent format, how to find freedom in the chaos of game day! Champions and winners have developed a plan on how to prepare for and expect success, and overcome challenges. Now you too can learn how to hold the trophy!"

*John Harris, U.S. Amateur Champion (1993); Champion's Tour winner*

"I was struck by Dr. Cook's *see it, feel it, trust it* teachings many years ago. It has affected the way I play the game, teach the game, parent, and lead my club. It will serve you well on all the 'game days' that are in front of you."

*Michael Leemhuis, CEO, Congressional Country Club, Site of 2011 U.S. Open*

"If you want to take your game to the next level, I recommend this book. Dr. Cook is one of the top mental game coaches in the business."

*Mike Adams, GOLF Magazine Top 100 Teacher; Golf Digest Top 50 Instructor; Director of Instruction Hamilton Farm G.C.*

"*The Psychology of Tournament Golf* provides a fresh perspective on golf whether you are a seasoned competitor or recreational golfer. We have applied Dr. Cook's ideas and highly recommend them to you."

*Tom and Lynda Case; Tom: Two time winner of the Florida State Mid Am; Lynda: Winner of the Florida State Am, Florida Sr. Am, and Southern Am.*

*David L. Cook*

# **DEDICATION**

To my wife Karen, the light and love of my life. You relentlessly inspire, encourage, and facilitate the audacious dreams of our family. And to my daughters, Lexie and Hannah, who refuse to accept ordinary while extraordinary is an option. Your lives call out greatness in your daddy.

# ACKNOWLEDGEMENTS

To my dad for putting a club in my hand and a shag bag by my side.

To my mom for showing me what unconditional love looks like.

To Jim Hardy for not only writing the foreword, but for being a friend who has been unwavering through the storms of life. You are a hero to me.

To Bob Rotella my Sport Psychology leader and mentor. It was a privilege to sit under your teaching. It is an honor to be part of your indelible legacy.

To the late Johnny Arreaga, my childhood golf pro, who first inspired my search for the psychology of tournament golf.

To Liz Worley for polishing my words with your impeccable copy-editing skills.

To Robert Wolgemuth for representing me as an author, challenging me to dig deep as a wordsmith.

*David L. Cook*

# FOREWORD BY JIM HARDY
## 2007 NATIONAL PGA TEACHER OF THE YEAR

I was excited when David Cook asked if I would write the foreword to his new book... excited and humbled. David is a dear friend, a fellow sports professional, and a mentor to me. He is a true mentor because of the manner in which he lives his life. David is both a seeker and follower of truth. He is an inspiration and a role model to me and to countless others. When the invitation came to join him on this new venture, my joy to help him was mixed with humbling concern; would I be up to the task.

David and I share many common interests and goals. Among them is our passion for excellence. In particular we have a passion for helping people enjoy and play better golf. Although coming from different professions within the golf spectrum--me from a swing technician perspective and David from a sports psychology position--we have often coached the same students. We have also taught together in clinics and golf outings. Our purpose has always been the same: to maximize a player's potential through both improved technique and performance.

Writing the foreword to this book is particularly exciting. It is my invitation to you to embark on a journey of discovery. First and foremost, you will find the answers you have been looking for on game day. Dr. Cook's game day mental approach will put your mind in position to succeed. You will find the information profound and useable. It will change the way you approach and play this great game. When you commit to these principles your game day performance will improve. Whether you are competing in the U.S. Open, the second flight of your club championship, or trying to win a $10 Nassau, this book is for you.

Secondly, David's books never stop with traditional status quo information; they always press the reader to go deeper. In the bonus sections of this book you will be moving forward into disputed and largely uncharted waters between two historically opposed positions. Think of those two positions as unfriendly nations with a gulf between them. One country is the home to the technical and mechanical pursuit of the golf swing while the other is the on-course, often under pressure, mental and emotional guidance needed to maximize your golfing performance. To illustrate this gulf, most golfers have heard the definition of the "hardest shot in golf"..."the one from the practice tee to the first tee."

The practice tee is where the majority of learned technique takes place. It's where swing doctors like me hang out a lot. It's where swings are broken down, analyzed, diagnosed, and improved. The practice range is where much of the repetition occurs that competitors need to hone their swings. Historically it's where instructors have urged golfers to single-mindedly concentrate on what is happening within their swings. To affect change or cause greater repetition, they exhort their students to block out any extraneous thoughts other than those pertaining to the exact swing prescription being employed. It is a technical lab. It's the shop where you bring your car to be repaired, or to be rebuilt for greater speed or better functionality over rough terrain. The mechanic is the president of this country.

Then the first tee is all about performance and playing the game in front of the ball. The car is no longer in the shop; it's now in the race. It's grinding over the outback. The president of this nation wants performance skill. He demands attention on playing the music not learning the notes. He wants you to feel and listen to the music and to dance to it, not to wonder what your feet are doing. He implores you to play golf not play golf swing. His desire is to have you take the skill you have rehearsed on the range and now perform with it in the midst of interference, pressure, and adversity. He implores you to visualize the target, to see the shot. He wants you to block out mechanical thoughts and allow yourself the freedom to respond to the demands of the game. He believes technical swing thoughts have a tendency to undermine a fluid performance.

I hope you can see the troubled waters between the two countries. It's why the hardest shot in golf is between the practice tee and the first tee. On the one hand, how can the golfer under the pressure of the first tee execute his newly rebuilt swing and not revert to the "old" mistake prone habit without focusing on at least one mechanical swing key?  Conversely, how can the golfer dance to the music, let alone even hear the music if he's concentrating solely on what his feet are doing?  This debate has been endless in golf. The two positions are too often at war with each other.

Dr. Cook and I have often consulted with the same PGA Tour players through the years. We have been in a sense co-coaches on the same team. The mutual respect we share has always been strong and evident, respecting what each brought to the table. We have worked together to find the timing when we felt the student had assimilated the mechanical changes sufficiently to phase out of technical golf into performance mode. We in essence found a way to bridge the gulf between the two nations. Even though our skills are different, we recognized the validity of each other's position and because of that we were successful.

I always wondered though, was there some way to better bridge the technical and mental. Was there some way to shorten the time barrier between the two?  Could you incorporate mechanical aspects into pure performance? I've always felt it was possible to meld the two traditionally unfriendly positions into one that was compatible as well as highly successful. In reading this book you will learn that it is not only possible, but also how to do it.

David has developed some groundbreaking thoughts on making this happen. You are about to discover the bridge. This information was first disclosed in his golf novels (*Seven Days in Utopia* and the sequel *Johnny's U.S. Open*). An in-depth explanation of this bridge is included in the bonus sections of this book. It has a chance to change the way you approach the game.

David was able to do this for several reasons. First, he is not only a highly respected sports psychologist with an incredible success record, but is also a highly accomplished golfer. I've known David for quite some time. I have watched his journey as he has moved from the traditional sport psychology stance to finding ways to accommodate swing keys into his student's game day processes. Experience has shown him that there often has to be a blending of the two.

It was David's pursuit of blending mechanics and performance in his own game that turned the tide for him. His creativity is immense and abundant. He is not afraid of new, different, and unconventional. In fact he thrives on it. He gets a kick out of helping people with traditional problems see the light with non-traditional solutions. David truly lives in both worlds, and because of that he has come up with an approach that on the surface seems unorthodox but produces totally correct and orthodox results. Results that reside in both worlds: better swing mechanics and improved mental game performance.

I know that you will easily adapt and appreciate the power of the mental game strategies in the first section. I also believe that if you let go of tradition and try the new swing idea and putting technique in the bonus sections you will be surprised. His purpose for including the bonus sections is to produce efficient and easily synchronized mechanics that translate into easier feel and rhythm under pressure, which makes the jump to the first tee effortless. In the end, that's his goal... to solve the hardest shot in golf. Who knows, you may be the first to win the U.S. Open (or your club championship) with the *Utopia Pre-Set* swing, or *Face-On* putting. It's by trying David's ideas that you experience moving thought to feel to action. Once you've experienced that, you're on your way.

*David L. Cook*

## INTRODUCTION
# WHY UTOPIA?

*I drove down the one-lane entrance to the Links of Utopia that had become so familiar this life-altering week. It was a "windows down" sort of road. You wanted to experience it, not just drive it. Unlike the entrances to the modern-day master-planned communities and country clubs, this stretch of road was flanked by the authenticity of life. Nothing was imported. Without the help of a gardener, native wildflowers bloomed in concert with the natural grasses and vines. Sensing their short-lived splendor, wildflowers sprang to life with a flurry and lived life greatly, knowing the slower-growing grasses would survive them in the coming heat. Cattle stared you down with the curiosity while chewing their cud, oblivious to the world outside of their fence. The century-old rusted barbed-wire fence served its purpose faithfully, held together by the stoic rot-proof cedar posts born in the valley. Obsessed by failure earlier in the week, I had been too preoccupied to experience life beyond the surface, missing what Monet lived to paint.*

Seven Days in Utopia, p. 103

Sometimes in life you have to take a trek to a simple place to discover profound truths. Utopia is such a place. It is a small village in the Hill Country of Texas where I have spent a lot of time contemplating. Revelations abound when we slow down the speed, turn down the noise, breathe deeply, and listen to the voice of wisdom that resides in such a place.

A revelation is a deeply intimate and divine treasure. It can't be planned; it has to be caught. It requires a heart of freedom and receptivity in a world that is staunchly entrenched in tradition. You have to be in the right mindset to catch it. Often this gift arrives in a most unsuspecting place.

Over the past few years I have been receiving *revelational* downloads on a driving range. Not just any range, an out-of-the-way range and nine-holer in Utopia, Texas. The course, which used to be a goat ranch, could kindly be called minimalist. It's setting, among the majestic oaks of the Sabinal Valley, is truly heavenly. It is a sweet spot for creative thought and audacious ideas. Utopia is the birthplace of my two novels and movie about golf, life, and faith. Its serene setting has become a destination for thousands of sojourners. They come seeking divine revelation. They leave deeply moved by the significance of their own story. The Utopia mystique has become an epicenter for revelation.

Thus this book is the third in a series that was birthed from Utopia. When I contemplate the essence of the two novels that preceded

*David L. Cook*

this book, I can clearly see that a new way has been birthed. The ideas introduced in the novels are indeed more than fiction. These ideas are truth waiting for the courageous to embrace them. There is something stirring in this out-of-the-way place. It just might be a golf revolution. You are being invited along on the journey. The answers you've been searching for in golf, business, or life just might be revealed within this series from Utopia.

Three specific golf-related elements have come out of my time in Utopia: *The Psychology of Tournament Golf*, anchored by *See it, Feel it, Trust it*; the *Utopia Pre-Set Swing*; and non-anchored *Face-On Putting*. Collectively, they create a seamless *revelational* approach to game-day performance that addresses both mental and mechanical aspects of this great game. While I introduced them in the novels, I will unpack them in a practical and applicable manner in this book. I strongly recommend that you read the two novels to have a context for what you are about to discover in these pages. You can find your copies of *Seven Days in Utopia* or the sequel *Johnny's U.S. Open* at www.linksofutopia.com.

On a personal note, I have fully incorporated each of these three elements into my own game. I am undeniably a better player today as a senior amateur than I was in college on a golf scholarship.

## CHAPTER 1
# THE QUEST

*"Here's a thought for you that will serve you well on your journey."* Johnny proceeded to share one of his many simple but profound quotes: *"Always set an extra place at the dinner table, so when destiny comes knocking at your door you invite him in as though you have been expecting him."*

*Johnny had a way with words. He also had a way with timing. In the silence of the next twenty seconds as we walked to the ball, this quote sunk deep, touching and inspiring the source of greatness, a seed that had been sown earlier in my life but had failed to be watered. It was a seed born out of childhood stories of valor and heroism, knights in shining armor, and warriors riding upon white horses. The hero was always prepared. When his number was called, with much confidence and skill he struck down his foe with great expectation of victory. In my heart of hearts I wanted to be one of them. But somewhere along the way, I slammed this door hearing only the voice that said, "You are ordinary; extraordinary is only for the books." But this week a story was being written, and expectations were increasing.*

*Seven Days in Utopia, pp. 117 - 118*

*David L. Cook*

When I was 14 years old, I was out on the course with my golf pro, the late Johnny Arreaga. He was on his way to shooting a 61 on this particular day. He was a player. On number 17, a par three of about 160 yards on the now-defunct Woodland West Country Club, Johnny knocked it up there to about a foot for birdie. He returned his club to his bag and said, "Picasso."

He was famous for saying that after a good shot. It was his trademark. Johnny believed golf was an art and that every shot started with a blank canvas. He taught me that we open the door to greatness when we choose to paint a masterpiece. He always signed his painting, "Picasso."

This was my introduction to the mental game of golf, the first secret to playing my best when it meant the most. I later discovered that when we fail to choose to paint a masterpiece in important performances of golf or life, we are left to deal with stick figure outcomes.

Johnny taught me the second secret on the range. Like most of you, I loved to practice as a kid. I couldn't hit enough balls to satisfy my insatiable desire to get better, to find the sweet spot yet again. The sweet spot is an addictive force. It is the true motivation behind the game. I hit balls all day long, shagging them on our makeshift range. Each ball was like gold to me. I had retrieved most of them from the snake-infested murky waters of number 7 where my buddies and I waded barefoot into the neck-deep water, feeling for balls with our toes. I marked them carefully with a magic marker and washed them often. These pond-retrieved treasures became the foundation of my quest for success.

I was in heaven hitting balls. There were few days during the summer when my friends and I didn't hit a bushel of balls and play at least 36 holes. We carried our bags and often broke in club members' stiff leather golf shoes for a buck or two on our hunt for par.

We only had a handful of junior tournaments in those days. Junior golf was just getting organized. Our intensity around tournaments was high, knowing that we had just a few opportunities to post a score for our world to see. That is how we discovered that game day was different than every other day. Interference lurked around every corner, pressure mounted with every shot, and the fear of failure emerged seemingly out of nowhere.

I often came home from a tournament dejected and beat up. Johnny was always there to help pick up the pieces. It was frustrating to have so much potential on the range and in practice and yet on game day fail to reach that potential. He would graciously meet me at the range after a tournament, knowing my world had just ended. Without asking a word about how I scored or what went wrong, he would ask me to hit a few shots, focusing on rhythm. He would ask me to swing at about 85 percent to create the feel he was after. Next he would talk to me about balance. He'd stop my swing at different points and push on my body from the front and back and side to get me centered. Finally, he would ask me to be patient in the transition, almost pause at the top. He said I was so anxious to see the outcome of the shot on game day that I failed to finish my swing.

Before I knew it, I was stripping the ball. I had found the sweet spot once again, and life was good. At that point Johnny would ask me, "So, what's the problem?"

I learned from this great man that no golf swing was perfect. We all have compensations in our swings. But great players find the secret to synchronizing their compensating parts under pressure. Johnny taught me the second secret to playing my best when it meant the most by helping me find rhythm, balance, and patience.

Rhythm, balance, and patience, along with envisioning a masterpiece, became the first two mental keys for me on game day, thanks to those early lessons from Johnny. They gave me the strategies I needed to have freedom in the chaos on game day.

Armed with Picasso as well as rhythm, balance, and patience, I began my search for "The Psychology of Tournament Golf." Nearly four decades later it is my privilege to share the lessons of my journey. I know that I am but a product of my mentors like Johnny, PGA golf instructors, Tour players, fellow competitors, and professors in the field of applied sport psychology. I am honored to stand in the shadow of their legacies.

This book lays out the timeless principles of game day psychology that I have learned, researched, and taught. These principles have changed the destinies of many players, including myself. I have written in a succinct, no-nonsense fashion, leaving plenty of space for your personal notes in the margins, so you can carry the book, review it often, and use it as a game-day primer over and over again as you pursue your tournament dreams.

Wear out the cover of this book. Freely write notes in the margins of the text, dog-ear meaningful pages, and pen notes on the journal pages at the end. The book is small enough to be stored in your golf bag, readily available as a map to greatness for all the game days in your future.

My goal is simple: to have you *play your best when it means the most.*

*David L. Cook*

## CHAPTER 2
# "TWENTY MINUTES BEFORE THE TROPHY CELEBRATION"

> *"Mental chaos has stolen more majors than players want to admit," Johnny answered. "Freedom has to trump chaos coming down the stretch. When destiny is on the line, defining moments are characterized by thought freedom, meltdowns by mental chaos."*
>
> *Johnny's U.S. Open, p. 30*

Tournament day is different than every other day. It is fraught with interference and is a cauldron of pressure and intensity. Your mind is bombarded with distractions, not the least of which is the posting of a score. The first thing you realize early on is that physical talent isn't going to get the job done by itself. Potential just isn't enough on game day. You need more.

The second thing you realize is that hitting thousands of balls on the range doesn't guarantee success either. While there is no substitute for practice and honing your swing, I'm going to go out on a limb and say that golf is the worst practiced sport of all. Raking and hitting five-iron after five-iron on perfectly level and mown grass to an area without any ramifications fails to consider what awaits on the first tee. People are watching, gamesmanship commences, wind is howling, OB appears to the left, water shimmers to the right, and the pin resides 600 yards in the distance without a level lie anywhere between the tee box and green. What's more, there is a score to be posted.

The first step toward playing your best on game day starts with a couple of pictures. First, you have to see yourself holding the trophy. You have to have the audacity to believe in victory. It is a choice that must happen. It provides an inspired focus for the journey. In reality, you can't win them all. But when you do emerge victorious one day, you will know that the seed to victory was in the picture you chose.

If during the course of the tournament, victory becomes out of reach, redefine your goal, in essence, your trophy. It might be top 10, making the cut, etc. The trophy becomes a metaphor for playing for something high and great on game day. I just left a tournament where my player was in the hunt early then fell out of contention along the way. On the final day it would have been easy to cash it in. Instead we re-worked "the trophy picture" for him. He was in 48th position and we set top 30 as the new trophy. He bought in and was ready to get after it. When the round was over, he had posted a 5 under 67, having moved up 26 spots. Not only did he have a smile on his face and more money in his pocket, his low round of the day was fuel for the next event.

The word *volition* is defined as "the will to choose." The spectrum of volition goes something like this: I won't, I can't, I'd like to, I'll try, I can, I will. Every moment in your life, you will make a choice within your mind, and this choice will have startling consequences upon your performance. The first choice of greatness is to choose nothing less than, "I will."

With that said, I am finding that players need a second and even more important picture. It is a clear and real vision of what it will look like about 20 minutes before the trophy celebration. That is a place of tremendous thought storms that can potentially steal a victory and, in some cases, halt a destiny.

To hold a trophy (or reach your goal) you have to walk through the 20 minutes before the trophy celebration. Mental chaos will be raining down. Up by one coming to the home hole. Tied in a sudden death playoff. A downhill, slick–as–glass twelve-footer for victory. On the cut-line with two to play.

Being strategically ready for dealing with success is critical. How many worthy players have risen to the top of the leader board on the final day only to crash in a heap of ashes, unprepared for the final climb to the summit, the 20 minutes before the trophy celebration?

Early in my career I had a young aspiring mini tour player come in for a session. He told me his story. At one point in his career he had won a prestigious National Amateur tournament that got him into the Masters. He had always dreamed of playing in some Tour event one day. He just skipped a few rungs in the ladder by receiving this invitation to one of the grandest of them all.

He practiced hard for months on his game. Hit lots of balls. He felt like he was prepared with his physical game when he showed up. But he was not prepared for what was about to happen on the day the pairings came out. He was in shape, had learned the course, his swing was under control, and he was as comfortable as could be expected. Then it happened. He saw his pairing and nearly fainted. He was paired with his childhood idol Jack Nicklaus. Jack was still playing well and would be followed by thousands. This young man's goals changed from playing one shot at a time to two prayers: Dear God, let me be able to get the ball on the tee on the first hole. And secondly, don't let me kill a spectator on the first drive. Ultimately he shot an 81 the first day and spent the day, in his words, "trying to stay out of Jack's way and not throwing up on myself."

On day two the traditional repairing took place and he went out in the first group with another amateur who had shot an 81 with Arnie. It was early in the morning, no spectators around, and they both shot even par 72 on day two.

The question that has to be answered is this: What was the difference between day one and day two? To start with, it wasn't talent. It wasn't potential. The difference was the amount of perceived interference. They were not ready mentally for the challenge.

When he shared that story, one of my life's missions was cemented firmly into my soul: Don't ever let my students get into situations for which they aren't mentally prepared. Like a good pilot instructor, I want my players ready for the emergency. I never want to hear a young player say what this player said as he concluded his story, "I wish I knew then what you are teaching me now. The outcome would have been very different. I may never have that opportunity again."

In the end, freedom in the chaos will be your greatest gift on game day. Pulling off the shot of your life starts here. It requires taking the time to prepare your mind for the battles ahead, including the inevitable 20 minutes before the trophy celebration.

*David L. Cook*

## CHAPTER 3
# PRE-GAME

> *"Armed with a new perspective on life and a revamped mental game, I anticipated the round like a lion waking up hungry and ready to hunt. With no fear of failure, I headed in my car for a new destiny. There simply is no power in life like having the right competitive perspective coupled with a bulletproof mental strategy. For the first time in my life, my compass was pointing to true north… I wrote a script for the next day's round. While the course was familiar, I wanted to be ready when the spikes went on. My script described two goals: Keep the game in perspective, and see it, feel it, and trust it on every shot."*
>
> Seven Days in Utopia, p. 139

**First thoughts**:

The first step to winning the mental game battle on tournament day is to start the day rehearsing your round in your mind's eye. I call this "scripting" and in fact it may help for you to write it out. Keep it to about a page if you write it out so it doesn't become overwhelming.

*David L. Cook*

Before your foot touches the floor, lie in bed and think through the day or read your script. Think through your warm-up at the range, defining and seeing your purpose accomplished. Walk through your strategy on the first three and last three holes and imagine yourself pulling off the shots to accomplish your goal. Most of all focus on your mindset and mental process, the one thing over which you have 100 percent control. Speak about it in your mind, have conviction for mental toughness and a bulletproof mindset, and commit to the plan set out in this book. See Chapter 8 for how to use the "great shot journal" and the "mental toughness journal" for pre-game confidence.

**Warm-up on the range:**

When you arrive at the course, head to the range—not to practice, but to warm up. These are two different assignments. Practice is about working on and honing a skill. Warming up is taking what you have on game day and finding rhythm, balance, and patience. Your body will be on point and in a state of readiness. I call this a "super state." You likely will have a level of adrenaline unlike the day before, coupled with tension and an elevated heart rate that comes with it. It is easy to let this take you out of the game. With increased heart rate and tension, the physical outcome is usually "short and quick," which causes off center shots at the least and hooks and blocks at the worst.

*Psychology of Tournament Golf*

The key to warming up in the long game is finding a means to managing this new energy, the super state. You don't want to get rid of all the new electricity; you want to use it to your benefit. To do this, it is imperative to focus on rhythm, balance, and patience on the range. You may have to use thoughts like "long and slow" to find the sweet spot. Your mind has to adjust to the increased energy. When it does, you will be ready. The focus isn't on hitting perfect shots; it is synchronizing your compensating parts with the increased energy of game day. That is your goal during the warm-up.

Finish the long-game practice session by hitting the first two shots you will need on this course. Paint the picture on the range, swing with the feel you just discovered, and leave the range ready to attack your target from the first shot.

**Practice Green:**

Your goal on the practice green on game day is for finding the feel of the green, not making putts. To find the feel for the green, you have to putt long putts. Find a spot where you can putt to a target 20 feet away, then 30, then 40, and finally 50. Go back and forth between those distances until you feel the green. I like to use painter's tape or bright chalk line string to lay out a section about 4 feet wide. Move away at the distances above and putt your ball to stop on top of the tape. You will be putting for distance, and distance is

*David L. Cook*

feel. Aiming for the tape, rather than the hole, is key to having your brain focus on the feel of the green. Not until you have the feel for the green, having your ball roll consistently, will you be able to read a green. In essence most every putt is a speed putt, so rolling the ball the right distance consistently allows you to read putts well.

There are two variables in putting: distance and direction. Warming up is about finding distance. And in the end, distance is the more important of the two variables to becoming a great putter. I heard one of the greatest putters on Tour once say, "All I think about is putting the ball in the generally vicinity of the hole with the right speed, and sometimes they fall in. Distance is everything."

Having time on the green where your brain is free to let go of direction will engage the gears of feel to a level needed to produce results during competition. If you can enter game day with more of your brain focus going to feel, good things have a chance to happen. At the very least your ball will always be around the hole.

Finally, finish your session on the green by making a few two and three footers to hear the ball going into the cup. That is a good sound with which to leave the putting green.

Use the same idea for chipping and pitching. The idea is to really click in on the firmness and speed of the greens.

## CHAPTER 4
# GAME TIME

*I moved in behind the ball. My senses were fully engaged, as I had been painting the scene for the better part of an hour. I saw the aiming point, shape of the shot, and trajectory. I could see the base of the flag, my final target. The shot line was encased in red.*

*As I moved into the shot and addressed the ball, I felt the shot. My club waggled as if something inside were testing the waters. The ball was back in my stance with the clubface slightly open. My feet remained dynamic as I almost danced into final position. As my eyes returned to the ball, the memory was etched in my mind. The club moved off the ball as I trusted the shot. Freedom ensued....*

*I stood there, taking it in. Johnny didn't say a word. In a real sense I had just stepped back into my childhood. I was at play, and art was my companion. And it felt right."*

*Seven Days in Utopia, p. 69*

What am I supposed to think over a shot? This is many golfers' ultimate question. The answer may surprise you: *see it, feel it, trust it.*

*David L. Cook*

These powerful words accomplish all you need to put yourself in position mentally over a golf shot. Your main job during the round is to put your mind in position to succeed over each shot. In other words, play one shot at a time. To do this, you have to have a bulletproof thought process to which you are committed.

There is a concept in psychology called the law of recentcy. It basically states that during a performance your body will respond aggressively to the thoughts it receives most recent to movement. In golf, I identify this as the final 10 to 15 seconds before the club moves. During this time frame, put a shield around your thoughts by actively focusing on the process: *see it, feel it, trust it*. This becomes your missile defense system against random thoughts that want to disrupt your concentration.

Many thoughts will weave in and out of your mind during a round. A negative thought isn't harmful unless you dwell on it. When thoughts come, identify them as simply a thought, not good or bad. Don't give them power, just identify them as all vanilla. When you don't agree with or like the thought, don't attempt to block it. Instead, let it go and replace it with another. If you don't like the thought of a lemon, think of an orange. If you try to block out the lemon, it will only get bigger. I will explain this in more detail later in the chapter.

When you choose to aggressively pursue a thought, that in and of itself blocks other less desirable intruders from undermining your potential. The question then becomes, what thoughts. Counting to four or choosing some random word or phrase to battle negative thoughts works to a degree, but I am going to have you choose the most powerful self coaching words in existence. There is nothing random about our choices. They each have a purpose; they all are critical elements in the success chain.

## SEE IT

> *"I learned long ago that golf is to art like dance is to music,' instructed Johnny. "Dance is a physical expression of the music; a golf shot is a physical expression of art..."*
>
> *"To be a great player, you must be a great shot-maker. To be a great shot-maker, you must become an artist."*
>
> Seven Days in Utopia, p. 64

The first element is to create a masterpiece, to *see it*. Instead of coaching you to visualize the shot, I want you to remember three one-word prompts. Visualizing a shot is not a specific-enough command to battle the thought storms during the "shot of your life."

*David L. Cook*

You must have a bulletproof process that is specific, tangible, and easily accessed in the heat of competition.

Think of a pilot trying to land a plane in the fog. Your muscles represent the pilot attempting to access information that will allow him to pull off the landing. The air-traffic controller doesn't ask the pilot to visualize the plane slightly turning to the left, slowing down a smidgen, and lowering the nose a bit. Instead the air-traffic controller gives very specific information in terms of compass heading, airspeed, and angle of attack. This information is critical. It is the difference between life and death.

Here are the three words that define *see it*: target, shape, and trajectory. Target is your landing point. Shape is the route the shot will take to its landing point. Trajectory defines the height of the shot.

**Target:** This is the specific ending point for your shot. You will adjust your alignment off this reference point according to the magnitude of the shot shape that you choose as dictated by wind and slope of the ground.

Very often the target in competition is not the flag or center of the fairway. I heard that Ben Hogan was once asked why he hadn't made a hole in one in PGA tournament competition. His reply was quick and telling, "I seldom aim at the flag." His job was to put the shot in position to make a birdie. That meant hit it below the hole so that the percentages on making the putt were in his favor.

It is important that you spend a good deal of time aiming at objects other than the flag on the practice range. You have to train your eyes to align to objects on the ground, mounds, trees in the distance, or even clouds if they aren't moving too fast. One of my favorite teachers in Dallas tells his students to look up in the air for targets rather along the ground. I like this concept because that is where the ball is traveling and presents a realistic picture to paint.

I have worked with players who were "flag bound." Their instincts were so ingrained at hitting to flags during practice that they had a mental battle hitting away from the flag during competition. One particular Tour player was tied for the lead with two holes to go. Number 17 was a par three with water right and a moderate wind blowing left to right. The pin was cut right. His natural shot was a slight fade. He hit it in the water to lose his chance for victory. After the round he said that he tried to aim way left but his body wouldn't believe him. He was flag bound, and it cost him.

Years ago I met one of Jack Nicklaus's former caddies. He told me that Jack's question when they reached the tee on a par four or five was always the same, "Where is the pin today?" He asked this back on the tee box because he was a master at playing the angles.

He chose spots in his landing zone that would give him the best angle to the flag, thus gaining on the field by strategizing better. The greatest player to have played the game always started with a specific target.

**Shape:** Most every shot will move in one direction or the other because of wind or shot pattern. The greats typically eliminated one side of the course in terms of misses, thus increasing their odds for success. They did this by knowing beyond a shadow of a doubt which way the ball would be curving. In my estimation, playing a consistent ball movement in one direction or the other is central to confidence. The hardest thing in golf is to hit a perfectly straight shot. Not knowing if it is going to lean or move one way or the other is a doubt-producing drain.

To play this game at the highest level means you have to be a shot-maker. Shot-makers are made not born, and to become one requires volition. You have to reserve time during tournament preparation to specifically practice for creativity. Most players have a preferred shot pattern, which I support and encourage. But the best players can pull off any shot almost at will.

Falling in love with a single shot pattern is fine. But if you can't hit all the shots, this love affair can be the death knell to a player aspiring to be great. I have seen players who draw the ball refuse to hit a cut in a right-to-left wind with water left. Something in their belief system has identified the needed shot as an "inferior shot" it seems. They won't give themselves permission to hit the shot that has the greatest chance of hitting and holding the fairway or green. Somewhere in their past they fell in love with a shot rather than playing the game in front of them.

I can remember distinctly walking up to a par three in practice with a guy who had his name on his bag (i.e., a pro), wind whipping off the right, lake right with the pin tucked right, and out of bounds to the left. He looked over the situation and said to me, "I don't have a shot." I half-jokingly said, "You need to get rid of that Tour bag then." We spent an hour on that hole until he understood how great he really was.

He had to embrace the variables and dig deep to hit a shot that somewhere down the ages his dad had taught him was inferior. He realized how easy it was to hit a cut against the wind and how lightly the ball would come to rest. He learned that it was not changing his swing, just adjusting the face angle, his alignment, and ball position. It was as though he was let out of prison. He came to love the fade so much, it became his go-to shot on the Tour. He rapidly climbed the money list in the months that followed. He became a confident shot maker.

Practicing on a course, or scrimmaging as I call it, is the best way to practice shaping shots. It produces situations that are real, that engage creativity and imagination.

**Trajectory:** The height of the shot determines how the ball will react to the wind and landing surface. Trajectory is such an important variable in shot choice. It becomes even more imperative in a recovery shot mode to be able to manipulate it low and high according to the situation. You want to know that you know you can pull it off before the tournament begins. When you make a decision in competition, you can have no doubt in your mind. You have to believe and have confidence at that moment.

I worked with a prominent rookie Tour player a few years back who had no answer to the "tweener" shot or how to keep it low into the wind. When I asked him what happened to his ball when he choked down, he said that it had little effect on his shots. So I asked him to show me. He choked down about half an inch or so and proceeded to prove there was no difference. I then asked him to give me a one-thumb length choke-down on the grip (about three inches). He explained, "The club feels too short like that."

I said, "It's the same length as your wedge, and you hit that club OK, don't you?" He agreed and hit a few shots. Trajectory was significantly lower and it went about eight to 10 yards shorter. He tried it with several of his irons and learned a valuable lesson about changing trajectory and hitting the in-between shot without working at it. Moving the ball back in his stance and forward with the one-thumb length choke down also altered the trajectory, spin, shape, and roll. All of this without working at it produced many new and needed shots at his disposal on game day.

We make the game too hard sometimes. Exploring every conceivable shot in practice produces confidence. It brings great revelation, exponentially increasing potential.

It's no wonder guys like Seve Ballesteros, who started playing with only one club for every shot, excelled in the creative aspects of the game. They were fearless. Specialty shots inspired them. They had so many shots up their sleeves that it took the pressure off their long game. They were confident in their recovery abilities. I still hit plenty of Chi Chi punch-and-run bunker shots with 9 and 8 irons when faced with across-the-green sand play. Chi Chi Rodriguez was a magician at using different clubs from the bunkers.

Shots we don't typically practice are the shots we define as difficult. Pressure often has its origin in a poor definition of the shots we face. On the volition scale it comes from "I can't" or "I'll try" decisions. Every shot is simply point A to point B. There is a shape and trajectory that will get it there without over-trying. If not, then it is a chip out or an unplayable and we move on.

When I walk inside the ropes on Tuesday or Wednesday with a player, we often play "call your shot." The player gives their caddy permission to not give them a club until they verbally call their shot, making themselves fully accountable to the shot. Calling a shot means focusing on the three elements above: target, shape, and trajectory.

One of the greatest stories of my career as a sport psychologist happened to me when I was working with a Tour pro who had missed five cuts in a row coming into this particular tournament. He was frustrated after changing his lifelong swing. The decision to change had been based on casual comment made by a broadcast announcer about how he "should" be doing it. The outcome: he was trying to hit spots in his backswing, rather than take dead aim at the target in front of him. For two days we returned to his previously solid swing and shot pattern, and we played Call Your Shot. He gave his caddy permission to not give him a club until he called his shot: target, shape, and trajectory.

It was as though he was freed from the prison of doubt. I have never witnessed such a ball-striking display. Amazing transformation. As we approached the ninth hole during the practice round, his caddy reminded us that this was the playoff hole in this tournament. I asked this player what shot he would hit if he were in a sudden-death playoff on Sunday afternoon. His initial response was half joking, "I've missed five cuts in a row... not sure we need to worry about that."

In other words, he didn't really believe he deserved to think about winning. Like many players he believed that only those who finished high in the previous tournament could have the audacity to think about winning. We talked it through, and I got him to thinking that he is never more than one swing away from entering the zone. In fact, his shots that day were proof. He agreed and chose to believe that anything was possible. Then he described in detail the shot he would hit on this demanding golf hole.

Sunday came and so did the zone. He ended in a tie. Off to number nine these two non-winners went for a sudden death play-off.

With a destiny on the line, my player called his shot to his caddy just as he had on Tuesday. He pegged his ball with conviction and blistered a low, boring, trapped three-metal left-to-right slider to the center of the fairway.

It was now the other player's turn. Right before he took it back, he balked. He went back behind the ball and started over. The commentators were all over this, speculating on what he was thinking. He approached the ball timidly, swung timidly, and cringed as he watched his shot feather into the water hazard. The reporter on the course reported that he had hit the same shot earlier in the round or would have won this tournament outright.

The reason for the balk on the drive was most likely the memory of that earlier shot. While I never talked to this player, it seemed that all he had in his arsenal was to say, "Whatever you do don't hit it in the water again." Trying to block out a bad image only makes it bigger and more influential. If you try not to think about a lemon, it only gets brighter and more sour. You can taste it. Blocking isn't going to get the job done. Instead you have to replace the lemon with an orange. In golf terms, you have to call your shot. Become deliberate and intentional about what you are going to do, rather than blocking against a shot you don't want to hit.

Both of these players' lives were changed that day. The player who had missed 5 cuts in a row walked into his destiny because he had freedom in the chaos: He chose to call his shot. He had committed to that freedom in his pre-game plan and practice. From Tuesday on, he practiced and played, expecting to be in a playoff. The other player won a few years later, using this experience to prepare him for the 20 minutes before the trophy celebration. He was blessed to have another chance.

To summarize: To *see it* is the first step in the mental process over a shot. Painting a masterpiece is the object, and calling your shot accomplishes the task. See the shot before you pull the club and again behind the shot.

## FEEL IT

> *Fly-fishing is all about rhythm, balance, and patience. It is an art. The fish becomes secondary. It takes a calm mindset focused on the feel of the motion rather that the outcome. Johnny was cleverly recalibrating my internal feel and profoundly changing my approach to golf.*
>
> Seven Days in Utopia, p. 55

Once you have called your shot, your muscles are starting to interpret the image sent to them. They are beginning to feel it. You now step into the shot and allow the feel of the shot to cover you top to bottom. By repeating the words *feel it* as you take your stance and look to the target, you are setting the wheels in motion. You have the option of taking a practice swing or waggle, your preference.

*David L. Cook*

The objective is to create a sense of rhythm, balance, and patience. You have called the shot. You must now put your muscles into position to pull off the shot. Body awareness is critical. Tension is deadly if you don't combat it with this stage. You will naturally feel the heat and be aroused with a faster heart rate and tension in the heat of competition. Never assume that the feeling of extreme butterflies means that you are about to fail. Just the opposite. It simply means you are in a super-state and can pull off more physical strength with less energy. Therefore, reining in the emotion by consciously walking slower, releasing your grip pressure down to a 5 from a 10, waggling the club slow and smooth, keeping your feet and body moving and dynamic as you align for the shot, breathing deep, keeping your teeth apart (we carry more tension here than almost anywhere) are strategies that will make this super-state work in your favor.

Listen carefully to this point: The biggest failure in the *feel it* step is trying to get the shot over with. Golf is a great game. We play it to find the sweet spot, to enjoy the moment, to savor every shot. You must patiently and expectantly approach each shot with confidence. I have worked with so many players who have a shot they don't like or a club they are currently having difficulty with (i.e., putter, driver, wedge). They will hurry to see the outcome, thus undermining the whole idea of the *feel it* step.

You may look down at the ball and back at the target as needed. This step is genuinely about releasing the muscles to feel the shot. Concentrate on rhythm, balance, and patience. You may have a swing key here that helps as well. Great teachers ask you to "feel this" when teaching you a new or old move. Feel releases you to the next stage of trust. You cannot time feel; so don't worry about the number of looks. But make the final look a gunfighter look. Stare it down. When you are ready, let your eyes move to the ball for the final step.

## **TRUST IT**

> *"Do you see the progression?" he asked. "First, you must see; second, you feel; third, you trust. Trust is the epitome of golf. It is the freedom to swing and let go. Great athletes compete best when they are free. Trust, you see, is earned. It is earned by feel, and feel is earned by seeing. Therefore, art is the catalyst to a great shot."*
>
> *Seven Days in Utopia, p. 65*

The final step in the process is to let it go, *trust it*. Trust is the moment you release your muscles to do what they have been primed to do. You have seen, you have felt, now it is time to let go. Trust is the trigger to start the swing. It is a feeling of freedom rather than forcing, being settled rather than anxious. Trust is a decision of the heart, not based on previous outcomes. It is a decision at a moment in time to let the body freely do what you just coached it to do. There are no hitches. There is no guiding or over-controlling of the swing. It becomes a dance with a sense of rhythm and grace.

Trust doesn't have to be the complete absence of mechanical control, but it bumps right up against it. It is the definition of freedom. Your body works best when it is free and unencumbered by too many mechanical thoughts. Through the years I have come to understand that for most players to trust their swing, they have a swing key or mechanical trigger word or feel to initiate the swing. This is normal. I just like the idea of 80 percent of the focus of a shot to be in front of the ball and 20 percent behind the ball. On your best days, when you enter the zone completely, you will pay little attention behind the ball. You will dance and not count your steps. (note: in the bonus section you will find an approach to the swing that was developed to keep the game in front of the ball.)

Trust is earned by feel, and feel is earned by seeing. Trust is the open door to getting into the zone. It doesn't guarantee success, but it sure puts your mind and body in position at a moment in time for greatness to emerge. That is all we can ask of ourselves.

*Psychology of Tournament Golf*

After you take the final look, return your eyes to the ball. As they meet the ball, repeat the words *trust it*. The club should move off the ball within a few moments of your eyes meeting the ball. Your work is done; it is time to dance.

You want to move the club off the ball quickly for two reasons. First, you don't want to become static. You want to keep your feet, the club head, and your hands moving, hitting the ball from a dynamic start rather than a rigid start. You can be still for a moment or two, but staring at the ball for several seconds is not the precursor to freedom.

The second reason to get the club moving is because the masterpiece dissipates the longer you look away from the target. You want to stay connected to the picture, especially on the short game. Game day is about playing the game in front of the ball.

Players fail to trust for four reasons. I call them the errors of trust: pressing, guiding, over-aiming, and jamming. These principles are based on research done by my good friend and colleague Dr. Bill Moore (www.drbillmoore.com).

**Pressing:** Pressing is defining the situation as critical or overly important. It is adding anything to a shot other than point A to point

B. Once you find those two points, and the shape and trajectory to get the ball there, everything else is pressing. Thoughts like, "This is really an important shot," or "I really need this," or "this is critical," or "this is a hard shot" all undermine trust. They cause us to press, and pressing undermines freedom.

**Guiding:** Guiding is the second error of trust and is defined as playing away from trouble rather than to a target. Thoughts such as, "Whatever you do, don't hit it out of bounds," or "I can't miss it there," also undermine trust. *See it, feel it,* and *trust it* lead you to attack a target, not play away from trouble. You can be the predator or the prey. To win on game day, you have to be hunting targets, not running from poor thoughts.

**Over-aiming:** Over-aiming is the third error of trust and most often happens on the green. When you attempt to putt a ball down a string, it tends to tighten your muscles, causing tension rather than freedom in your stroke. You end up creating an impossible margin of error that causes you to become line-bound. Remember, there are two variables in putting, distance and direction. When you become line-bound, you undermine distance because feel is compromised. When line-bound, your focus is monopolized by the fact there is no margin for error.

I encourage players to create lanes in their minds eye. I like the idea of a 10 percent margin of error. Create a lane that has a width about 10 percent of the length of the putt. On a four-foot putt, the margin is just about the width of the hole. On a 10-footer, the lane is one foot wide. When your object is to putt the ball inside the 10 percent lane, you feel free from over-aiming, you focus on the distance, and your feel is enhanced.

I also firmly believe in putting the ball to stop at the back of the hole. That is different than hammering the ball into the back of the cup. The hole is the biggest when the ball is rolling the exact speed to stop at the back of the hole. The faster the ball is moving at the hole, the smaller the hole. If it is moving where it will stop just at the back of the hole, the ball has a chance to fall in the front, sides, and back of the hole.

**Jamming:** Jamming is the final error of trust and happens when there is too much controlling going on in the mind. Jamming happens when you over-instruct your muscles what to do, rather than trusting the painting, your feel process, and a simple swing key. Golfers mistakenly believe that during a tournament they must be in total control of the intricacies of their entire swing. On the range, we hit shots mindlessly, and our body responds with great shots. Yet we go to the tournament thinking, "This is for real, so now I have to bear down and tell my entire body what to do." Trust is the freedom to minimize the chatter and let it happen.

I had a player a few years back who declared that he couldn't putt. He had just had 42 putts in a mini tour event. He was humiliated and incredibly frustrated. I asked him to throw down a couple balls on the green while we were talking. I had put a string on the green about 30 feet away that was three feet wide. While we were shooting the breeze, I asked him to see if he could stop a ball on top of the string. While we were still talking, he hit his first putt within a half an inch of the string and dead center. He had never seen nor putted on these greens. They were a different surface than he had just putted on in the tournament.

Then I surprised him by calling him a liar (I had a smile on my face). I said no human could do that without having incredible talent. I told him that he wasn't a poor putter at all; he was a poor thinker. He was a master at the errors of trust. That was the last putt he hit during our lesson. He had his best finish the next week, because he learned what it meant to *trust it* rather than pressing, guiding, over-aiming, and jamming.

To summarize, *see it, feel it, trust it* is a process that is bulletproof. It puts the mind in ready position and allows trust, the essence of great golf, to be earned by feel and feel earned by seeing. Research has proven that this is how the mind works best in this sport.

Let me end this section with a story. I can remember a day of reckoning in my sport psychology career. A golf-pro friend of mine introduced me to a crusty old no-nonsense Tour Player with years of success under his belt. This weathered warrior was nearing the end of his illustrious career. He was still hoping to compete at a high level on the Champion's Tour and was looking for help with his driver. He had lost his confidence off the tee. He was an accomplished short game player who had a line of putters and wedges with his name on them. The three of us teed off the first hole in a friendly round to get to know each other. The Tour player proceeded to snap hook his first drive deep into the woods at which point my dry wit, and courageous golf pro, said in a loud voice, "And that is why he doesn't have his name on a line of drivers."

Later that day I earned the right to share the *see it, feel it, trust it* process with this player. He embraced it and committed to it with his driver. We moved toward the green where I wanted him to incorporate the routine into his short game as well. When he set his bag down next to the green, he looked at me with his piercing eyes and without a smile said, "I am one of the greatest short game players of all time. Do you really expect me to use this process with my putter and wedges?" I was caught off guard but had no choice. "Absolutely," I said wondering if he was about to laugh and walk off. Instead he smiled and said, "Good, I was just seeing what you would say. This is exactly what I have always done in my short game, just hadn't been able to put it in words. Lets get started."

Obviously I breathed a sigh of relief. But more than that his response revealed that *see it, feel it, trust it* was not something new. The greats have used it for years. We are just putting words to it.

## CHAPTER 5
# ACCOUNTABILITY TO THE PROCESS

*"The reason for the concentration score," Johnny explained, "is for accountability to the process. People say they are going to change, but without accountability, they seldom do."*

*Seven Days in Utopia, p. 106*

I have two practical suggestions for controlling the one thing you can control on tournament day, your thinking. When implemented, they become like game day coaches.

**SFT:** The first suggestion is the ball itself. Mark your ball in two places with the letters SFT. We need reminders that coach us as if we had a coach with us. Now every time you look down at the ball, it is coaching you to leverage your potential on game day. This becomes your first game day coach. I can guarantee that it will make a huge difference. It will keep you accountable to your goal no matter where you find your ball.

I can remember teeing it up once in the state amateur well into my career at that point. I had made it to match play. My competitor walked up to the official and said, "I am playing a Titleist 1 with SFT marked in two spots." He then looked at me with a smile as he confidently walked by to tee off and said, "I've been to the seminar." That made me smile.

**Concentration Scorecard:** My second suggestion to control your thinking is to keep track of your concentration score on your scorecard. After each hole, write down your outcome score as always. Then somewhere in the same square as the outcome score put a second number, your concentration score. If you had an outcome of four on the first hole, ask yourself on how many of those shots you went through the SFT process; if all four, write a four in the box. If only three, write that number. Count tap-ins and penalty shots as concentrated, so your score isn't incorrectly skewed negatively. Understand, this score is not based on the outcome of the shot, rather on the input before the shot. The SFT process doesn't guarantee success; it just puts you in position for success to happen more often. Follow this assignment on each hole. This becomes your second game day coach.

Your goal for the day is to put your mind in position to score on each shot. All other goals fall under this one goal. Every stat improves as your concentration stat improves.

At the end of the round you can divide your concentration score by your outcome score and get a percentage. This percentage is the most telling stat of the day. It reveals the percentage of time you put your mind in position to succeed. If you get above 85 percent, you are doing well. It is a difficult but worthy goal, and one that guarantees that you have given yourself the best opportunity to succeed over each shot. You have heard, "Play one shot at a time." Most likely no one has taught you practically how to do that. Your concentration score is a true and objective measure of this subjective idea.

As you review your card, you will be able to identify the shots where you failed to accomplish your goal. This will help you identify the situations when your concentration waivered. Knowing this information will help you win against these hot buttons in future rounds.

Finally, your concentration score holds you accountable the entire round to your goal. If you mark your ball with SFT and keep your concentration score, you have a great chance to have freedom in the chaos on game day.

One of my first students was a mini tour player. He aspired to play on the PGA Tour. For five years he had unsuccessfully attempted to qualify at Tour School. We met a few weeks before he was to play in a PGA event on a sponsor's exemption. He committed to the *see it, feel it, trust it* process. He also committed to keeping track of his concentration score on his scorecard. When the tournament was over, he emerged as a PGA Tour winner with a two-year exemption on the PGA Tour. He had reached his dream. He shared his scorecards with me and they revealed that he was over 90% with his process. That day this dedicated young man walked into his destiny because he had freedom in the chaos. Among other things, keeping his concentration scorecard kept him focused and allowed him to play his best when it meant the most.

## CHAPTER 6
# THE THREE-CHALLENGE CONCEPT

*Inside I finally began to see that game day was about preparation, not only for the swing, but for the environment ripe with emergencies. I had a new template, a new perspective and I knew that I had failed to completely prepare in the past. I had not had the mind-set of preparing for the emergencies.*

*Seven Days in Utopia, p. 97*

Now that you know what to think about over a shot and how to play one shot at a time, let's turn to reacting well to wayward shots. Putting your mind in position to score over a shot certainly helps eliminate wayward shots. However, golf is a tough sport with so many variables that you will invariably deal with failure, frustration, and the ball landing in less than desirable spots. Sometimes it is a poor swing; we aren't perfect. Sometimes it is a misjudgment of wind, distance, or club selection. Other times it is an unfortunate bounce or other environmental effect. Whatever the issue, you have to deal with it effectively. To win on game day requires mental toughness in the face of challenge. We have to be ready for the emergencies.

*David L. Cook*

One of the most effective tools that I use with players is what I call the three-challenge concept. It is a concept, which means it is based on truth, but not absolute truth. Here is the idea. We need to expect success; that's why we create a masterpiece. But we also have to be ready for the "what if" scenario at all times, especially coming down the stretch.

My first lesson with a pilot instructor ended with an emergency landing. Not that we had one, he just created one to teach me a lesson. After the lesson he said that by law he could not sign me off to fly a plane until I was ready for an emergency. For the next 40 hours of flight instruction we practiced every conceivable emergency until I was supremely confident that I could get the plane back on the ground safely. I realized I was really paying for crashing lessons, not flying lessons. I came to understand, that to enjoy and be capable of flying, I had to be ready for an emergency.

That is what the three-challenge concept is all about. I have told several young players that I would not sign them off to play in a tournament until they were ready for the emergencies. When you embrace this principle, you will separate yourself from the pack on game day.

For a good player, the number of major challenges in a round averages about three, thus the three-challenge concept. This is just my observation, which is why it is a concept and not fact. In every round of competitive play you are likely to face and overcome three major challenges. A major challenge is any situation that can alter your focus and derail your round. Finding your ball in the center of the fairway in a deep divot, finding your ball resting in a footprint or poorly raked bunker, having to take an unplayable, hitting any shot that costs you a penalty, being put on the clock, having an annoying playing partner, a rain delay, or having your ball hit a sprinkler head near the hole. These are just some of the examples. You have plenty you could easily recall.

If you know everyone is going to be challenged three times, you won't think, "Why does this always happen to me and never to anyone else?" We eliminate that excuse right away.

Secondly, if every competitor is going to face challenges, it means that part of victory is overcoming the challenges better than my competition. It inspires you to see this as an opportunity rather than a failure to moan and groan about. You can actually get excited about winning the recovery game.

Thirdly, it will motivate you to practice for the emergencies. Get off the flat perfectly manicured range and begin to practice recovery shots from every conceivable situation. Understand that practicing recovery shots is essential to scoring better in those challenging situations.

Write "3 Challenge" on the top of your scorecard so you see it all day long. Along with marking your ball with SFT and keeping your concentration score, it is your third game-day coach: keeping your focus and attention in check during the intensity of the round.

## CHAPTER 7
# "FAKE IT 'TIL YOU MAKE IT"

You will have days when you show up at a tournament feeling as far away from being a champion as possible. During those times you have to know that you're never more than one swing away from finding the zone. Your head will open the door to moving to the next great round. Don't wait for something good to happen; make something good happen. Sometimes you just have to fake it 'til you make it.

I had an aspiring Champion's Tour player tell me that if he could only putt, he could make it. To him, putting was holding him back from accomplishing his lifelong dream of earning a spot on the Champions Tour. He was a club pro and top instructor at the time.

I was leading a session for other club professionals on putting, and he was there to support and give credibility to my words. We were between groups and had a few minutes to kill on the putting green. I asked him, if he could putt like anyone in the world, who would it be? He chose Curtis Strange, who had won a couple of Opens in a row. I challenged him to audition for the part, to become Curtis for the next 10 minutes. I told him I was a director of the movie looking for someone to play the part. To my surprise, he took me up on it.

For the next few minutes he putted brilliantly. His method didn't change as much as did his posture, grip-pressure, and rhythm. He looked at me with surprise. I challenged him to stay in character. After a while he stopped, amazed. Then I asked the question, "Was that you or Curtis Strange putting?" He looked confused for a moment but learned a great lesson. It was him, of course. He had just set aside the heavy weight of the false identity he had allowed to steal his true identity and talent.

We are all actors according to the thoughts we have. We can believe and act like a champion and open doors to greatness. Or we can look at stats and believe they tell the whole story and that we are stuck back in the pack. This great gentleman made a four-foot putt one year later at the Champion's Tour Qualifying School to secure the final spot on the Champion's Tour. The next time I saw him I called out his name. He looked at me and said, "It's Curtis Strange to you!"

I worked with another player who had the goal of becoming a member of the Champion's Tour. He had spent his life as a club pro as well. At one point he came home bellyaching yet again about his putting. His wife was done with it. She made him promise to look in the mirror at least three times a day, when he was brushing his teeth, combing his hair or dressing and simply say this phrase, "I can putt, I can putt, I can putt." He took the challenge, and his life changed. He not only made it on the Champion's Tour, but he made millions of dollars and played for more than ten productive years before retiring. He was known by his peers for his great putting. His wife made my job easy.

What may seem like faking it is often our talking ourselves into believing we are champions.

*David L. Cook*

# CHAPTER 8
# COURSE MANAGEMENT

*Day one of the U.S. Open shocked the world. The course reminded me of freshman chemistry where the grandiose plans of many a student came crashing down, relegating them to second choice majors.*

*Never had the scoring average been so high and flameouts so prevalent. The water had been cut back the day before, leaving the fairways and greens rock hard. The narrow fairways were cut so tight that players had to read the break from the tee box and play clubs to the flat spots. Only those who had taken the time to notice and chart these areas during the practice rounds were surviving.*

*Johnny's U.S. Open, p. 127*

There are two other scores that you should consider keeping as well. I don't want you to be overwhelmed, so begin with your concentration score only. Then add these two as you can. Eventually it will become easy, almost second nature. And when it does, you will be playing a different game than you are today.

QP: QP represents quality position on the green. You earn a QP on your scorecard if your ball comes to rest in regulation within 20 feet (about seven steps) of the hole and is below or situated within this distance with a fairly flat putt. This score is more telling than the number of putts taken during the round. This score represents the number of high-percentage putts you had during a round. It is a pretty good measure of legitimate birdie opportunities during the round.

I have had an endless number of players falsely accuse their putting as the culprit to a poor round leading to a loss of confidence with the putter. When investigating more closely we found that they spent their day putting from outside QP: Long putts, significantly downhill, or putts with large breaks. No one's putting can stand up to that kind of pressure in the long run.

At the end of the day, they failed to choose or execute well enough to reach QP targets. The outcome, they falsely blamed their putter leading to a loss of confidence with the flat stick and it snowballed from there.

Strategically choosing specific targets on the green is imperative. Keeping the ball below the hole increases the percentages of makes, even if the ball comes to rest off the green. QP is a great goal for a good player.

Remember Hogan's point earlier in the book. He said that hitting the ball in position to have a birdie putt was more important than aiming at the flag.

QA: QA is a measure of quality angles into the green on par 4s and 5s. Hitting a ball with an opening to the front of the green creates a higher percentage opportunity than one with a forced carry over water or a bunker. This is especially true in U.S. Open set up conditions. This is a subjective scoring system that you will have to create. QA1 is the best, QA2 is doable but not the best, and QA3 is a low-percentage angle.

As I mentioned earlier in the book, Jack Nicklaus asked his caddy about pin placement before he hit his drive, thus allowing him to narrow his target to a QA1 position if it were available.

At the end of the day, a lot of QPs and QA1s and QA2s will increase your opportunity for shooting a quality score. You can lower your scores without hitting a shot by using a strategy to outthink your opponents. Angles increase margin, and margin is a good thing in this unpredictable game.

I was getting ready to play in a state open a few years back. I played a practice round with a former champion, who made an astute observation. He said that players who shoot for the middle of these greens would be in a fight all weekend long. The reason, he said, was that the greens were all crowned and that from the center of the green players would have downhill curlers for the most part. As I observed carefully during the round, I understood. On this course hitting to the center of the green wasn't the best strategy. There were few QPs to be found in the middle of the greens on this course. To succeed in this event I had to choose carefully and strategically.

## CHAPTER 9
## FUN

*"Son," he implored, "you have a choice. If you choose to trust me and let yourself enjoy this game, you just may see greatness unfold. It is your choice…"*

*Once again his words cut to my heart. As a child learning the game, I had been free and uninhibited. Days were filled with wonder and shot-making adventures. Learning was ever-present and a three-putt was just that. A score was a goal, not a definition of a man's self worth.*

Seven Days in Utopia, p. 108

*We entered the zone of pure and undefiled fun, the foundation of backyard sport. It is a shame that organized sport has stolen the heart and imaginations of our children. The word sandlot has become obsolete in a generation in need of magical moments.*

Johnny's U.S. Open, p. 156

*David L. Cook*

Tournament day should be fun. I love watching Phil Mickelson play golf; his grin says it all. He loves game day, even if he isn't on top. Somewhere along the way we got it backwards. We have fun in practice and hit great shots, letting it go, trusting it, and playing great. But on game day we think we have to be serious, sour looking, and in control every swing. It doesn't take a rocket scientist to understand the correlation between fun and good performance.

Game day should be the moment you have been waiting for. It's the chance to "dance for the world" as Sarah Hughes said after she shocked the world and won the gold medal in Olympics figure skating a few years back. She explained that she had always dreamed of how wonderful and fun it would be on game day to skate and dance for the world. Her competitors all crashed and burned from fear of failure. She had fun; they looked like deer in the headlights before they competed. The others hoped that their performance might turn out well, thus turning a miserable day into fun when it was finally over. She brought fun to the game.

I believe you have to escort fun to the course. It is a decision of the heart. Some players have told me that they can only have fun when they are playing well. That is conditional fun, based on performance. Fun has to be a choice, not a conditional response to some subjective measure against par. When you are having fun, your muscles will work their best. Sure, there is intensity and pressure, but the process described in this book takes about 15 seconds over every shot. The rest of the time can be a walk in the park, a place of great anticipation and fun. Game day is what you have worked for. Enjoy it.

*David L. Cook*

## CHAPTER 10
# POST ROUND GAME DAY

*"By the way," he taught, "the only thing more powerful than calling your shot is recalling a shot. What you just did is recall the shot from Wednesday. Always savor your shots, so you can take advantage of this most powerful tool in your armor, the recall."*

*Seven Days in Utopia, p. 119*

There are two things I suggest for post round analysis. You should keep both of these in a journal that you will carry with you to every tournament site and add to through the years. Eventually you will fill several journals with great content from your experiences. I have left plenty of blank pages at the end of this book to double as your first journal.

**Great Shots Journal:** Think back to a shot or two that were particularly memorable during the round. Write out in detail a description of the shot, including date, course, hole number, club, distance, wind, obstacles (if there were any), shape of the shot, feel, and what it meant to the round. Use enough detail so you will be escorted back to that exact moment in your mind when you need it.

*David L. Cook*

I worked with a Tour player who eventually won at Pebble Beach. The first time on a course with him we were standing on a par 3. I asked what he was thinking over the shot. He said, "That's simple, I am thinking of the last great 7 iron I hit." He could see it, feel it, taste it, hear it, and more. The reason was that he had learned early in life to savor great shots so that he could pull them up in the future. He was a master at this and adapted very well to the *see it, feel it, trust it* process.

Another player, the one that won in the playoff earlier in the book, returned to the same tournament eight years later. When he reached the 17th hole, where he had eagled the year he won, he found himself in the fairway at the exact spot, six inches from the 206-yard sprinkler head. He looked at his caddy and said "déjà vu." They remembered the shot from eight years before that set up an eagle on this reachable par 5. He let it sink in and cover him. He then hit the shot of his life. As the ball was flying through the air, his caddy spoke one of the great caddy lines of all times, "If that ain't no good, there ain't no good!" His 6 iron shot went in the hole! He made a double eagle from 206 yards to finish second in the tournament and post one of the PGA Tour's greatest comebacks.

The ability to recall a shot is the most powerful tool in your armor. Savor the good ones; let the bad ones go.

*Psychology of Tournament Golf*

**Mental Toughness Journal:** This is the second section you will want to carve out in your journal. This will require you to review your concentration score on each hole of your scorecard. Look for the holes where there is a discrepancy between your outcome score and your concentration score. This process will identify where you allowed interference to take you out of your game.

From that data, think back and describe the situations that pulled your attention from the SFT routine. You can create three columns on the page for this. Column one is "situation," column two is "negative response," and column three is "mental toughness response." As you are making your entry, describe in the first column the issue that caused the negative response (i.e., 3 putt the first green). Secondly, describe what went on in your mind, your negative response (i.e., "I am such a pathetic putter," or "I hate these greens," or "There goes my round.") In the third column, write a mental toughness response that you will use next time (i.e., "Stay with SFT," or, "Trust yourself; you are a good putter," or "Be patient; there are plenty more opportunities," or "This is one of your three challenges; answer the bell," etc.).

This journal becomes a huge player in your game-day success in the future. On the morning of a tournament round, read through some of your great shot entries. Through the years you will have hundreds, so just randomly flip through and read a few. This engages your mind to the possibilities and builds confidence about your true potential and talent.

Secondly, read column three of your mental toughness journal and fill your mind with powerful responses to the realities of the game. This will establish toughness in your mind for the emergencies of tournament day. Eventually you will catch yourself before or during a negative response during tournament play and choose a different response. You will begin to do this instinctively, knowing if you don't you will be making another column 2 journal entry after the round!

What you will find is that you will be adding significantly to the greatest shot section and less to the mental toughness section through the seasons of your career. You will also become aware of where your buttons get pushed, your tendencies. When you overcome your tendencies, you step into greatness.

## CHAPTER 11
# CONCLUSION

*"Well then it's simple. Adversity is strewn along the path that takes you to greatness. It makes your roots go deep. Challenge is the unexpected gift on the way to being mature and complete," Johnny revealed. "It's this uncommon perspective that provides freedom in the chaos. Very few competitors really get this."*

*Johnny's U.S. Open, p. 31*

This is such a great game and I am thankful to have grown up around it. It is also a privilege to encourage players like you as you seek your dreams. And I agree it is a hard game to master. There will be plenty of adversity along the way. Thought storms and naysayers will try to take you out. But now you have a plan.

A Tour player that I have worked with for a few years recently sent me his ultimate goal. No it wasn't to win a major. His goal was succinct and clear and profound. It simply said: *To put my mind in position over every shot so that I have the greatest chance for success at that moment in time.*

He got it. He understands. It is profound because every other goal in golf falls under this umbrella. He will have better stats, higher finishes, more wins, more money when he controls the one thing that initiates every shot: a thought. It is the one thing of which he has 100% control as well. It is the antidote to adversity in the process of becoming a mature and complete player.

He now has a way to hold himself accountable to that goal, and so do you. *See it, feel it, trust it* becomes the embodiment of his goal. Committing to the process over every shot, writing SFT on the ball, keeping track of it on the scorecard takes the mental game from subjective to objective. The mental toughness journal follows up and serves as a constant course correction for the long journey. The three-challenge concept provides an outlet for the realities of the game. The great shots journal continually points you to the truth: there is talent in there just waiting to come out. Sometimes you just have to "fake it til you make it. And finally fun is the choice that must be made if you are going to stay motivated through the years.

My goal for you: *play your best when it means the most*. Take this book and keep it in your bag and refer to it often. Make notes in the margin, fill up the empty pages with journal entries, and put your mind in position to score over every shot. When you do, you will see glimpses of greatness emerge.

I have added a bonus section for the curious. I have always believed that there was an approach to golf that would mesh the mental and physical games seamlessly. If you are willing to push the envelope a little, I think you will be intrigued with the next two sections. You are invited to explore with me an approach to the swing and putting that I believe brings the mind and body together in a more efficient and effective manner, thus helping us all to *play our best when it means the most.*

*David L. Cook*

## BONUS SECTION I
# THE UTOPIA PRE-SET
### A REVELATIONAL APPROACH TO BLENDING THE SWING AND THE MENTAL GAME

## CHAPTER 1
# FINDING THE SLOT

*"I believe that somewhere in the evolution of the competitive golf swing we missed an important point. The point is freedom during the chaos, intensity, and interference of game day. It is mental freedom that will allow the golfer to maintain focus in front of the ball where the game is played, where a masterpiece is painted, not behind the ball, where the player is trying to manage positions with an increased heart rate and tense and agitated muscles. As tension mounts, breakdowns in synchronization are inevitable. Panic takes the mind to the backswing rather than the target. Great players crash and burn as they emerge on the U.S. Open leader board, but not because they are poor players. They fall because their synchronization fails; they simply can't consistently get it in the slot coming down the stretch. They lack freedom to play the game in front of their ball when it means the most."*

*Johnny's U.S. Open: Golf's Sacred Journey 2, p. 39.*

David L. Cook

I had a revelation early one spring morning in Utopia. I was lying in bed before the sun came up, contemplating the writing of the sequel to *Seven Days in Utopia: Golf's Sacred Journey*. I thought back to an encounter I had with the great Harvey Penick on the driving range of the old Austin Country Club back in the late '70s. My dad and I were competing in the Texas State Father-Son Championship.

I had spent my life swinging the club with a shut face on the back swing. I had never gotten the club in the proper slot at the top. I had not learned how to pronate the toe open and hinge my wrists correctly. As you can imagine, I moved the ball strongly from right to left. In college I had what my teammates affectionately called the "Cook Hook." It was a few degrees worse than a duck hook.

Right before this particular tournament with my dad I had had enough. It was time to learn how to get the club in the proper slot. On the range one day I took the club to the top and stopped. I adjusted everything. I got the toe vertical and my left wrist hinged without being bowed. Once I got in position, I swung down from there without a backswing. The hook immediately disappeared and my shots were flying true, but a little shorter than normal. I was OK with that improvement, because straight was not something I was familiar with until that day.

I decided to suck it up and play that way in the State Father-Son. I was an anomaly on the range. However, Mr. Penick, the beloved pro at the host club, walked up to me on the range and asked about my swing. I explained what I was trying to accomplish, and he was delighted. He said, "Sonny, that is how I taught the backswing back in the day. You will do well with that swing."

He smiled and walked away, leaving me with the confidence to stick with it. I played well, but I was still missing something. I was losing distance, and my swing got steep. But I had lost the "Cook Hook" forever, and that was a good thing.

I eventually moved past this experiment and incorporated the new position at the top with a normal backswing motion. I was out of duck hook prison. While I was committed to the *see it, feel it, trust it* process, I began to play with one swing thought as well: get the club in the slot at the top. While my swing and scores got better, my focus, like that of most players I work with these days, was still too much on the backswing rather than playing the game in front of the ball. I had more work to do.

A few years ago I found the missing ingredient. Through a divine appointment I met Jim Hardy, who became a best friend and confidant to both my family and me. We were teaching a clinic together.

*David L. Cook*

I was teaching the mental game, and he was teaching the swing. I was fascinated with his ideas and propositions about swing plane. He talked about the one-plane and two-plane swings.

In less than five minutes of listening to his remarkable wisdom, I realized that the missing ingredient to my swing was getting it on a slightly flatter, or one-plane, swing path. For the next few years I did just that, and my game continued to improve. But I felt as if my focus was still too much on the backswing.

I am a part-time competitive golfer and full-time sport psychologist, among other things. I began to understand that getting the toe pronated just the right amount, the club precisely on plane, the wrist hinged just right while keeping the back of the left wrist flat, all while maintaining the correct spine angle while all the parts were in motion, was a monumental task for a part-time competitor. To hit the slot and synchronize all the moving parts time and again, especially in competition, was going to be a continuing issue for me or for anyone who competes in this great game. With the traditional swing, this game takes enormous maintenance to be competitive. Getting the club in the slot under pressure takes practice and experience. And, as I have discussed previously, it takes a bulletproof mental process.

On this early morning in Utopia all the pieces came together. There had to be an easier, more efficient way to get the club in the slot while allowing the player to maintain focus on the game in front of the ball. If we could find that secret formula, millions of frustrated players would find relief. The game would become easier to teach and play. Learning would accelerate. Performance for the amateur and pro alike would improve. That's when it hit me. The revelation was delivered.

I couldn't wait to try it out. I had discovered the key, though it was just a thought at that moment. My fear was that if this worked, it would be going against years of tradition. But I knew this: Tradition is safe only when it is based on absolute truth. In this case, tradition may have sold us short.

*David L. Cook*

## CHAPTER 2
# RE-ORDERING THE SWING COMPONENTS

*"Here you go. It's you time," Johnny said with great anticipation as he handed me the club and stepped aside. "Understand this: We aren't fundamentally changing your golf swing; we are changing the synchronization or the order of a couple of the elements of the swing."*

*Johnny's U.S. Open, p. 44*

As in many of life's problems, a lack of synchronization is often the culprit. This is often the case in most athletic performances, especially golf.

Golf is a game of compensating parts. These compensating parts produce great shots when they are synchronized. If the synchronization is compromised, so is the shot. As a sport psychologist, I can say with confidence that most players fail coming down the stretch not because they lack talent. They fail because of synchronization issues caused by tense and agitated muscles. The culprit is thought storms that take them out of their game. The players have no freedom in the chaos of game-day pressures. That is the genius in the first lesson I learned from Johnny—rhythm, balance, and patience—his first keys to synchronization under pressure.

For years I have worked in concert with swing teachers to help players get ready for game day. The swing teachers get them hitting the slot. I get them to maintain their concentration so they can hit the slot under pressure and play the game in front of the ball. Conventional logic has led players to hit a lot of balls (muscle memory) and develop a bullet-proof pre-shot and post-shot mental routine to keep synchronization problems at bay on game day.

I have seen careers turn around after applying the two principles of working hard and thinking well. Players climb the ladder to success using this wisdom. There is nothing like watching a player break through a barrier and reach a new level of success. Watching the physical and mental come together is awe-inspiring.

But I have seen many more players struggle to accomplish their goals. They wake up on game day and can't find their swing or lose it mid-round. Synchronization is absent. Thought storms begin to bombard their minds until the *see it, feel it, trust it* routine has been washed away in a sea of fear. Survival instincts take over, tension increases, emotions rage, and another one slips away. So frustrating for the player. So frustrating for the swing teacher. So frustrating for me.

But I am on to something that is going to change the balance. Here is the secret: First, there is a more efficient order of the synchronization key chain. Second, when we identify the links of the chain and re-order them, a built-in rhythm is formed, which promotes freedom in the chaos. This allows us to both play the game in front of the ball and hit the slot at the top. In other words, this new method connects the mind and body seamlessly. More importantly, this approach doesn't change a person's swing; it simply changes the order of the components.

*David L. Cook*

## CHAPTER 3
# THE PRE-SET SECRET

*"I call this the Utopia Pre-Set. It is a four-count rhythm swing that takes care of getting the club in the slot in the first two moves of the backswing rather than in the last two moves. This is the key to synchronization while under pressure," Johnny said as he approached another shot. "Watch carefully. There is a purposeful rhythm to this swing. Remember rhythm, balance, and patience from your time here before?"*

*Johnny's U.S. Open, p. 43*

So let's delve into the mystery. As I was contemplating my swing on that morning in Utopia, I focused on the two key components of the slot at the top of the swing: the wrist hinge with a flat left wrist and being on plane. It occurred to me that pre-setting them at the top was a start but that pre-setting them in the first two moves off the ball was superior. This would allow a full coil that was missing with the Penick start from the top. Armed with the Penick idea and the Hardy teachings on swing plane, I discovered that a golfer could get the club in the slot in the first two moves of the backswing rather in the last two moves of the backswing.

*David L. Cook*

Because you are looking at the positions directly in front of you, you can see if you are in the slot. With the traditional swing, you have to turn your head, compromising your swing, to see your position. Another benefit to this modified approach is that you don't have to alter your swing, just the order of the parts.

Here are the four components of the *Utopia Pre-Set* (described for a right hander):

1. First, **hinge your left wrist** into the proper position, keeping the back of the left wrist flat. The wrist hinges slightly, moving the club vertically off the ball while the arms and body remain motionless. You will want to raise your arms. Don't. Keep them in the address position, motionless. When done properly, the shaft will be about parallel to the ground. (You will have a tendency to cup the back of your wrist the first time you try this. It is imperative that the back of the left wrist is flat. Don't be worried about where the toe of the club is pointing at this stage; focus only on getting the back of the left wrist flat.)

2. The second move is to slightly **pronate (open) the toe** to get the clubface on plane. I choose about 2 o'clock. You will have to experiment with your swing; it will be between 1 and 2 o'clock. Getting the club on plane becomes easy at this point. You simply follow where the toe of your club is pointed as you initiate the

*Psychology of Tournament Golf*

backswing. Another way to think about it is to take the toe of the club towards your right shoulder.

3. The next two moves are simply to **turn back** (toe of club toward the right shoulder) then **turn through** around your spine, keeping the spine angle the same throughout the swing. In the old days they called this move "turning in the barrel." I noticed that with the thought of turning as the only action needed, my body turn improved dramatically. It was easy without all the other information rattling around in my brain. My tendency to sway off the ball disappeared immediately. (See each position and the sequence illustrated at www.utopiapreset.com.)

I couldn't wait to try out this revelation. Could it be true? Could it really change the way the game is played? Since that first swing in Utopia, I knew I had discovered a treasure.

I quickly found myself speaking the components of the swing out loud in a perfect four-count cadence: "hinge, plane, turn, turn." It was explosive, bringing the mental and physical together. I knew at that moment that I would never go back to the old way. Here's why:

1. Once I get the club in the slot in the first two moves, the swing has been simplified to a turn. I can see the slot happen. I can easily self-correct because the movement happens before my eyes.
2. The synchronization issues have been solved. It is much easier to stay in sync during competitive golf especially when you need freedom in the chaos. The reason: you are not trying to hit the slot in the midst of your backswing while hinging, pronating, and turning.
3. The four-count process creates a built in metronome that resists the tendency to get quick and short under pressure. By saying, "hinge, plane, turn, turn" in a perfect four-count rhythm, focus becomes almost bulletproof. You can find a metronome smart phone app to keep you in rhythm on game day while warming up or on any other day on the range when practicing.
4. I have hit more pure shots with this move in the past few years than the rest of my career combined.
5. I can play as little as once a week or once a month and find the slot instantly. It happens right in front of me. This will make the game easier for millions. My game is more consistent, as my handicap index indicates.
6. The *Utopia Pre-Set* is the only method I have witnessed that literally brings the mental and physical game together in one process. And that's the whole point.

## The Four-Count Rhythm:

*He set to his target, eyes painting a masterpiece. As his focus returned to the ball, he began an audible metronome-like count using the words hinge, plane, turn, turn as he striped another shot looking as though he was dancing to a four-count rhythm with a club named Ginger Rogers. He continued this dance with the future of golf for the next 10 minutes. With each shot he audibly spoke the words, holding himself accountable to an impeccable metronome like rhythm. The club effortlessly hit the slot each time. I was in awe. Never in my life had I seen such a display of complete swing control. While different-looking, the rhythm, balance, and patience of the four-count method was mesmerizing and intoxicating, a true athletic move with its own beauty.*

*Johnny's U.S. Open, p. 43 – 44.*

The most profound aspect of the *Utopia Pre-Set* is how it connects the mind and mechanics. I don't know of another swing that has accomplished that mission.

There are four components to the actual movement of the swing. First there is the wrist hinge. Secondly the toe is put on plane by pronating it to about 2 o'clock. Third is the turn back taking the toe of the club and moving it toward the right shoulder. And finally is the turn through. When done correctly these create a perfect four-count rhythm, a dance. When we enter the zone, we are dancing.

This method doesn't contradict the SFT process that I advocated earlier in the book; it refines it. Here is what it looks like now:

1. *See it*: First, see the shot by standing behind the ball and calling your shot. Then walk into the shot and align to your aiming point, keeping the picture alive.
2. *Feel it*: Feel is defined by rhythm, balance, and patience. This is where the four-count rhythm of *hinge, plane, turn, turn* literally defines feel for this swing and incorporates each of the elements of rhythm, balance, and patience.
3. *Trust it*: Trusting the picture you've envisioned and the four-count rhythm is the simplified essence of the *Utopia Pre-Set*. The process allows you to "let" rather than force or try. It truly is the meshing of the physical and mental aspects of this great game.

**Shaping Shots:**

The *Utopia Pre-Set* has a built-in system for shot-shaping, using just two components. Once you have explored the amount of hinge and pronation to produce a straight shot, it is easy to work from these settings to create shot shapes.

There are two main variables in the *Utopia Pre-Set* that will alter shot shape. The first is hinging the club with a flat, bowed, or cupped left wrist (or, if you're left-handed, your right wrist). Hinging the club with a bowed left wrist will promote a draw or hook. Hinging the club with a cupped left wrist will promote a fade or cut.

The second variable that will alter shot shape is the amount of pronation. 12 to 1 o'clock should promote a draw; 2 o'clock straight; and 3 o'clock should promote a fade. That you get to see your positions is the best part. You can take your time getting them just right. This is much more reliable than trying to feel or adjust these positions at the top of your swing while in motion.

*David L. Cook*

# CHAPTER 4
# CONCLUSION

*"Fear," Johnny whispered as his eyes followed the flight of the majestic hawk towering above the valley. "Fear is the opponent. It keeps the common man from soaring. The fear of broken dreams, failed attempts, unfulfilled expectations. ... Yesterday's lesson was about fear at its core. You just might change the way golf is played. ... The Utopia Pre-Set will be a part of the future of golf. ... If you fear, you will fail and be laughed off the course. If you embrace the challenge, realize the call, and play with the passion and focus of a revolutionary, you will be trailblazing a new method for all who play the game this day forward."*

*Johnny's U.S. Open: Golf's Sacred Journey 2, Chapter 6.*

Fear and doubt are the opponents of truth seekers. It will be no different for you. Attempting a new, unconventional method will make you step out of your comfort zone. Thought storms will rage when you first attempt the swing, especially in front of people.

During the transition, take your time, letting the approach sink in. Yes, you will likely top a few at first. Yes, it will feel uncomfortable the first few times. Yes, you will feel self-conscious. And yes, you might forget the words, *hinge, plane, turn, turn*. But when it clicks and you find the sweet spot and the metronome rhythm, it will be like your first kiss.

When you try the swing on the course for the first few times, forget about your score. Instead, focus on maintaining the four-count rhythm. You will be pleasantly surprised at how much this synchronizes your swing. See how many quality shots you hit during the round. Give it a chance and you will walk into a more efficient and effective approach to the game.

To get a visual of the positions of the *Utopia Pre-Set*, go to www.utopiapreset.com. Study the pictures and experiment with amount of hinge and pronation. Experiment with flat, cupped, and bowed left wrist in terms of ball flight. Most of all, have fun and enjoy the process. Let it happen; don't force it to happen.

Finally, I encourage you to read both novels and follow the story of Luke as he embarks on a life-changing journey that incorporates the *Utopia Pre-Set*. You can find both novels at www.linksofutopia.com.

# BONUS SECTION II
# FACE-ON PUTTING
## A PUTTING REVELATION

## CHAPTER 1
## TRUTH VS. TRADITION

Have you ever rolled a ball across the green toward the hole? If you have, you probably faced the hole and rolled it underhanded. And if you've ever tossed a set of keys to someone, you probably faced them and tossed them underhanded. I would guess that both actions were natural and not pre-meditated.

Now picture this instead: Your friend is standing 10 feet away with his hand in position to catch the keys. You take a look at his hand and turn sideways, while putting the keys in the palms of both of your hands rather than one. Next you look to the side at the target then back down at your hands. At that moment you swing your hands back in a slight circular motion and fling them and the keys at where you remember the target to be, because of course you are keeping your head and eyes down.

Can you predict the outcome? Keep this visual in mind as we investigate the evolution of putting.

*David L. Cook*

I have a great appreciation for many of the rich traditions of the game of golf. Golf is a sport built on tradition. But I also have a passion for truth. Truth should always trump tradition, especially when it involves performance.

I have spent my life playing this great game, as well as coaching those seeking answers to golf's most baffling mental game questions. Although my reputation has been built around my expertise in sport psychology, I started my career as a competitive golfer. I understand deeply the importance of the mind-body integration in the search for par.

In my work with elite players, poor putting has been the source of most distress and heartache. Putting confounds, frustrates, and infuriates. The club that holds more players back from their scoring potential is by far the putter. That frustrated potential has driven my search for the truth about putting.

I believe the culprit is tradition. Not the rich traditions of the game but the traditional side-on, two-handed putting technique handed down through the years, one generation to another. I think this widely accepted approach to putting has kept us from the truth about putting.

I think about how the high jump was transformed overnight by Dick Fosbury and the Fosbury flop. He decided to go over the bar back first and never looked back. Every high jump world record since that date has incorporated his method. Pete Gogolak believed side-on was a better method for kicking a field goal in football. Now no football player kicks straight at the goal. Chris Evert was the first professional tennis player to hit a backhand using two hands. Now almost all tennis players have followed suit.

Tradition has had an insidious hold on too many players in golf. Players, who have been held prisoner by the old way, are slowly looking for a better way to putt.

*David L. Cook*

# CHAPTER 2
# THE PUTTING TRANSFORMATION

Before I introduce you to a brand-new way to putt, let's first look at how the transition to freedom has already begun. Over the past few decades the future of putting has begun to emerge, but its complete transformation is still under way. Along the way, the USGA and others have put certain restrictions on putting methods to protect the integrity of the game. Here are some recent tradition-breaking putting methods:.

1. The long putter was introduced as a way to anchor the grip against the body to eliminate excess movement in the stroke. Using a long putter also allowed for single-joint putting, transferring all the feel and movement to one limb. This mimics other fine-motor skills such as painting or writing. The long putter also encouraged the player to stand taller, promoting better overall vision of the putting line.

2. Left-hand-low putting emerged as an answer to the breakdown of the wrists through the stroke.

3. The belly putter gave players an anchor similar to the long putter, while allowing golfers to stay in their comfort zone by having two hands on the club.

4. The claw grip has many faces but basically has rearranged the lower hand so that it hangs in a more natural position, similar to a violin grip.

5. How the player looks at the hole has also undergone changes. A few players have begun to look at the hole while putting, thus putting to a target rather than putting to a memory. Looking at the hole while putting emulates other similar skills like shooting free throws, throwing darts, bowling, and horseshoes.

These variations, among others, in how we look at the hole and how we hold the putter have introduced critical pieces of truth in putting. One method that comes closest to the approach I am proposing was used by Sam Snead, who called it "side-saddle" putting. He faced the hole while continuing to use a short putter and look at the ball while putting. Snead introduced the croquet method as well, placing the ball between his feet. But the USGA quickly banned this variation.

## CHAPTER 3
# THE FACE-ON REVELATION

Let me introduce you to a revelational approach to putting. I call it revelational because, like the other ideas in this book, it came to me one day in Utopia, Texas. I was at a standstill when writing *Seven Days in Utopia: Golf's Sacred Journey*. The entire book had been completed but there was a hole right in the middle. Chapter 6 was blank. I spent about three months allowing a thought seed to germinate, which would eventually become the backbone of the story. It was the concept of truth verses tradition. I needed the perfect symbol in the story to illustrate the point. After watching some cowboys pitch washers, it came to me.

I call it *"face-on"* putting, coining the term in *Seven Days in Utopia*. It had previously been referred to as the side-saddle method. I call it *face-on* to distinguish this method as one where the golfer looks face-on at the hole while putting rather than down at the ball. *Face-on* putting is a USGA-legal, non-anchoring method of putting. It merges the best of each of the previously tried techniques. However, *face-on* putting doesn't build on the traditional side-on approach; rather it starts with a clean slate.

The traditional side-on approach to golf was established to create torque. In order to strike a ball with velocity, torque is the necessary means of force. But putting differs from every other shot in golf. Putting doesn't need torque. Torque is used for power, and putting has no use for power.

Putting has to do with accuracy. Accuracy is enhanced by the face-on building blocks: straight-line shoulder joint movement, binocular vision, a true in-line pendulum swing, and looking at the target rather than putting to a memory.

*Face-on* putting allows the golfer to face the target, thus taking advantage of three truths:

1. First, it puts the one moving shoulder joint in position to swing freely straight back and straight through, thus allowing the putter head to stay on-line throughout the stroke. Traditional side-on putting, by contrast, puts the two shoulder joints in position to swing the putter head in a slightly curved arc.

2. Secondly, *face-on* putting allows both eyes to look straight at the hole. Side-on putting causes one eye to be closer to the hole.

3. Finally, *face-on* putting allows the player to look at the target, not the ball, while putting. Putting to the object of focus is more effective than putting to a memory. Traditional side-on putting (and side-saddle for that matter) forces the golfer to putt to a memory instead of simply looking at the target.

*David L. Cook*

## CHAPTER 4
# FACE-ON PUTTING UNVEILED

*"These cowboys started with a blank slate. On that slate I taught them to putt looking at the hole with binocular vision while using their familiar washer pitching motion. From a physics standpoint, they have several advantages over tradition. Binocular vision allows a truer picture of the target and line. They have one moving joint instead of two. They use the shoulder joint in such a way that it swings the club in a straight line like a pendulum with absolute freedom. Unlike traditional putting, the putter is anchored at the top. And finally, their feel is focused in one hand instead of two. Can you imagine Monet painting with two hands on the brush?"*

*Seven Days in Utopia, p. 81*

*Face-on* putting requires a medium-long putter (approximately 45 to 48 inches). This length allows the player to stand in an athletic position while staying fairly upright for a greater visual advantage. Use a putter with an oversized, face-balanced head so that hitting the sweet spot is not an issue while looking at the target.

*Face-on* putting emphasizes one joint and one arm, simplifying the movement and focusing the feel. The shoulder socket in the face-on position is free to move in an uninhibited pendulum motion when the putter is gripped correctly. Gripped correctly, the thumb of the non-putting hand will be on top of the putter as a hinge. The remaining fingers are wrapped around the grip loosely. The hand is then placed away from the body (USGA conforming) with the non-putting elbow stabilized against the body. The non-putting elbow becomes the stabilizer as it is tucked into the body (a legal USGA position).

Place the putter about six to12 inches in front of and to the right of your putting side foot. I like to put my putting side foot forward slightly. By leaning slightly out toward your putting arm, your eyes will be behind the ball, thus giving you great vision of the putter, ball, and hole. You'll easily see the line to the hole from this vantage point. Keep your head looking forward and fight the tendency to turn your head sideways. Your height, coupled with the length of the putter, will determine how far you should lean forward. I like an athletic position with knees flexed, which seems to promote a solid hit on the ball. I experimented with this for years and have concluded that flexing the knees gets you closer to the ball and inhibits off-center strikes. The putting hand is placed somewhere between one and two feet below the hinge hand, creating a 90 degree angle at the elbow joint.

I like to hold the putter between the thumb and fingers like a violin bow. This keeps the tips of the fingers active, the primary source of feel in the hands. You can experiment with the index finger down and behind the shaft if that fits you better.

While making the stroke, you can either look at the ball or the target when learning the technique. Eventually you should focus on the target while making the stroke. But I have witnessed great putting by some who look at the ball, similar to the old side-saddle method. Prior to the stroke, look from the target to the ball and back, tracing a pathway for the putt. It is important that your eyes remain level and in a binocular position. I have found that I have to consciously refrain from slightly twisting and turning my head back to the old side-on position.

Looking at the hole while putting may be the single greatest mental advantage of this method. It also will take patience and commitment during the transition. Looking at a target verses hitting to a memory greatly increases your concentration. Staring down the hole while stroking the putt can't help but increase your focus and feel. I have found that those who look at the hole have impeccable feel for distance. Their day is filled with makes or tap-ins, a far cry from stressing over another three-foot come-back.

*David L. Cook*

In terms of the stroke itself, I have experimented with a long and flowing stroke as well as a shorter aggressive stroke that keeps the putter accelerating through the ball. While the long slow stroke looks nice, it causes two issues. First, the putter head may have a tendency to sway off line slightly. Secondly, there is a tendency to decelerate. A short, more compact movement keeps the clubface on line and keeps the club head accelerating through the ball, allowing a more accurate and assertive roll on the ball. For a detailed demonstration of *face-on* putting go to: www.faceonputting.com.

## CHAPTER 5
# CONCLUSION

I have no doubt that *face-on* putting can increase efficiency and effectiveness of putting. It brings the best of all the putting techniques together around truth.

Becoming a *face-on* putter will require three conscious decisions:

1. First, you have to value truth over tradition. The research is on your side.

2. Second, you have to value excellence over acceptance. You will be challenged by naysayers. Let your putting speak for itself.

3. Third, you have to commit to change, realizing any new skill requires practice and a little getting used to. The good news is that *face-on* putting puts you in better physical and mental positions so the change will be easier.

While I can't guarantee results, I can guarantee that you will increase your probabilities for success because you will have several new truths on your side. Also, because your eyes are on the target and because you have the freedom of an uninhibited joint, putting *face-on* is virtually yip proof, bringing hope to the thousands who suffer from this putting epidemic.

Breaking away from tradition is first and foremost a mental issue. It requires a mindset that is discussed in detail in the first part of this book. I appreciate and applaud all those who had the courage and confidence to break from tradition in the search for the truth, especially Sam Snead. It takes the heart of a revolutionary to bring freedom.

As I mentioned earlier, *face-on* putting originated with the novel, *Seven Days in Utopia: Golf's Sacred Journey*. If you have not read the book or seen the movie, please take the time to learn of the intriguing origin of *face-on* putting, from the small town of Utopia, Texas.

And finally if you are intrigued by the potential of this putting method, take a look at our *Face-On Putter*™ at www.linksofutopia.com. While most any medium-long putter will work, we have created a design with unique features specific to the *face-on* method.

I included *face-on* putting in this book because I believe it helps connect the mental and physical game. Putting is the source of more head games than any other aspect of golf. To position every aspect of your body more efficiently and to focus your eyes on the target completely changes your potential for success.

*David L. Cook*

# WRAP UP

My intentions have been to give you a workable plan for all the game days in your future. Control that which you have control over and you will enjoy success as you seek your dreams. As Jim Hardy mentioned in the foreword, I also believe there is a better way to approach the game that merges the mental and physical game seamlessly. I know I took a chance by including the *Utopia Pre-Set* swing and *face-on* putting. I would be a hypocrite if I hadn't. Pushing the envelope is a good thing if it leads to a more efficient route to truth.

It is now your turn to push the envelope in your mind. Carry this book in your bag and make lots of notes and journal entries. It will become your missile defense system against most of the game day adversities that are sure to challenge you along the way. SFT!

*David L. Cook*

# EPILOGUE
## THE FINAL FRONTIER

There was a time in my career when I thought that finding the answer to the mental game was the final frontier in the success chain. But sometimes in life the search for "the" answer only leads to another question. I believed that unlocking the secrets of the mind would complete the performance circle, but I discovered there was more—I discovered that the mental game was not the ultimate step but the penultimate step in the success chain.

For as long as I could remember there was this unsettledness that stalked me like a predator. It attacked most ferociously in the midst of failure. A poor shot, a missed putt, posting a score that wasn't reflective of my talent, failing to reach my expectations, losing a match, or having a meltdown resulted in a searing pain that went deep into the recesses of my soul. I noticed it in others that I coached as well. In fact it seemed to be universal. While following the mental game plan that I have presented in this book will dramatically improve scores, confidence, and success, it still doesn't completely kill off the predator—the fear of failure.

This relentless foe had to be defeated if I were ever to reach my true potential or lead others to this sacred ground. The search for the answer took me beyond the mind and into the heart. While scientists and psychologists will dispute that there is such a thing, all competitors know it exists. It has been said that the heart is the "wellspring of life," and you and I have experienced it.

The heart is where our true identity is found. It is a deep place. The secret to who we are and what we were made for emanates from this river of life. It goes largely ignored and because of this the predator wins far too many battles. We live as the hunted on a plain in the midst of a hoard of running fools.

The good news is you and I weren't born to be the prey, we were born to hunt. For me this revelation was the final secret. It is the answer to showing up on the first hole bullet proof and ready to rock. It is the source to an uncommon passion and zeal. It is the bedrock of competition in golf and life.

You see, what I discovered was that golf is just a microcosm of life, a shadow of a bigger game—a game with enormous consequences. To win the battle of either I had to go deeper than SFT over the shot. I had to be settled in my heart and secure in who I was first. I couldn't let a score define my worth and value in life. I had to find the bedrock to my great and true destiny on this sacred journey. So do you. Once you seek and find this answer, you will be a hunter, not the prey.

A great revelation happened during my pursuit. I found the deeper meaning of SFT. It opened the door to freedom in the heart and removed the debilitating effects of the fear of failure. I have penned the answer in *Seven Days in Utopia: Golf's Sacred Journey* and its sequel *Johnny's U.S. Open: Golf's Sacred Journey 2*.

Keep the journey alive and seek greatness. The final frontier is close. It is found one step beyond the mind—it is found in the heart. The stakes are high.

*David L. Cook*

# ABOUT THE AUTHOR

Dr. David L. Cook is one of the Nation's most respected mental game coaches and speakers. He was named by Golf Digest (2013) as one of the Top Ten mental game experts in golf and has worked with over 100 PGA Tour players. His first mental game golf novel, *Seven Days in Utopia*, became a major film starring *Academy Award* winners Robert Duvall and Melissa Leo. He served as president and chairman of the board for *Utopia Films*, the production company for the movie. He also co-wrote the screenplay and served as an executive producer. Dr. Cook's sequel novel, *Johnny's U.S. Open*, is being considered for a second movie. Other clients have included Fortune 500 companies, Olympians, National Collegiate Champions, NFL, MLB, along with multiple NBA teams including an eight-year stint with the *San Antonio Spurs* that included two World Championships. He served as Director of Applied Sport Psychology for the *University of Kansas* for 12 years (1984 – 1996) and represented the United States at the *International Olympic Academy* in 1988 in Olympia, Greece.

David is a *Baylor* graduate (1980) and received his Ph.D. in sport and performance psychology from the *University of Virginia* (1984). He and his wife Karen have two daughters and live in the Hill Country of Texas.

*Psychology of Tournament Golf*

# "PLAY YOUR BEST"
## WITH OTHER RESOURCES BY DAVID L. COOK

Visit Dr. Cook's website at **www.DavidLCookPhD.com** to sign up for the newsletter, learn more about retreats, and to schedule Dr. Cook for consulting and speaking engagements.

You can also order copies of all of Dr. Cook's books and other resources via his online store:

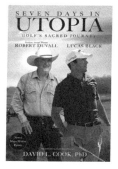

*Seven Days in Utopia: Golf's Sacred Journey*

*Johnny's U.S. Open: Golf's Sacred Journey 2*

*Seven Days in Utopia the Movie*
starring Academy Award Winners Robert Duvall and Melissa Leo

## DVDs

*The Complete Game* with Jim Hardy and Stan Utley

*The Mindset of a Champion: Performing Your Best When it Means the Most*

Order the *Face-On Putter* ™ exclusively at www.FaceOnPutter.com.

*David L. Cook*

# GREATEST SHOTS JOURNAL AND MENTAL TOUGHNESS JOURNAL

*David L. Cook*

Tournament site:

Date:

## Mental Toughness Journal:

| Adversity | Negative Response | Mental Toughness Response |

1.

2.

3.

*Psychology of Tournament Golf*

Tournament site:

Date:

**Greatest Shots Journal:**

1.

2.

3.

*David L. Cook*

Tournament site:

Date:

## Mental Toughness Journal:

<u>Adversity</u>     <u>Negative Response</u>     <u>Mental Toughness Response</u>

1.

2.

3.

*Psychology of Tournament Golf*

Tournament site:

Date:

**Greatest Shots Journal:**

1.

2.

3.

*David L. Cook*

Tournament site:

Date:

## Mental Toughness Journal:

Adversity        Negative Response        Mental Toughness Response

1.

2.

3.

*Psychology of Tournament Golf*

Tournament site:

Date:

## Greatest Shots Journal:

1.

2.

3.

*David L. Cook*

Tournament site:

Date:

## Mental Toughness Journal:

| Adversity | Negative Response | Mental Toughness Response |

1.

2.

3.

*Psychology of Tournament Golf*

Tournament site:

Date:

**Greatest Shots Journal:**

1.

2.

3.

*David L. Cook*


Tournament site:

Date:

## Mental Toughness Journal:

<u>Adversity</u>     <u>Negative Response</u>     <u>Mental Toughness Response</u>

1.


2.


3.

*Psychology of Tournament Golf*

Tournament site:

Date:

**Greatest Shots Journal:**

1.

2.

3.

*David L. Cook*

Tournament site:

Date:

## Mental Toughness Journal:

Adversity      Negative Response      Mental Toughness Response

1.

2.

3.

*Psychology of Tournament Golf*

Tournament site:

Date:

## Greatest Shots Journal:

1.

2.

3.

*David L. Cook*

Tournament site:

Date:

## Mental Toughness Journal:

| Adversity | Negative Response | Mental Toughness Response |

1.

2.

3.

*Psychology of Tournament Golf*

Tournament site:

Date:

## Greatest Shots Journal:

1.

2.

3.

*David L. Cook*

Tournament site:

Date:

## Mental Toughness Journal:

<u>Adversity</u>　　<u>Negative Response</u>　　<u>Mental Toughness Response</u>

1.

2.

3.

*Psychology of Tournament Golf*

Tournament site:

Date:

## Greatest Shots Journal:

1.

2.

3.

*David L. Cook*

Tournament site:

Date:

## Mental Toughness Journal:

Adversity     Negative Response     Mental Toughness Response

1.

2.

3.

*Psychology of Tournament Golf*

Tournament site:

Date:

## Greatest Shots Journal:

1.

2.

3.

David L. Cook

Tournament site:

Date:

## Mental Toughness Journal:

Adversity     Negative Response     Mental Toughness Response

1.

2.

3.

*Psychology of Tournament Golf*

Tournament site:

Date:

## Greatest Shots Journal:

1.

2.

3.

*David L. Cook*

Tournament site:

Date:

## Mental Toughness Journal:

<u>Adversity</u>     <u>Negative Response</u>     <u>Mental Toughness Response</u>

1.



2.



3.

Tournament site:

Date:

**Greatest Shots Journal:**

1.

2.

3.

*David L. Cook*

Tournament site:

Date:

## Mental Toughness Journal:

<u>Adversity</u>　　　<u>Negative Response</u>　　　<u>Mental Toughness Response</u>

1.

2.

3.

*Psychology of Tournament Golf*

Tournament site:

Date:

## Greatest Shots Journal:

1.

2.

3.

*David L. Cook*

Tournament site:

Date:

## Mental Toughness Journal:

<u>Adversity</u>　　　<u>Negative Response</u>　　　<u>Mental Toughness Response</u>

1.

2.

3.

*Psychology of Tournament Golf*

Tournament site:

Date:

## Greatest Shots Journal:

1.

2.

3.

*David L. Cook*

Tournament site:

Date:

## Mental Toughness Journal:

Adversity    Negative Response    Mental Toughness Response

1.

2.

3.

*Psychology of Tournament Golf*

Tournament site:

Date:

## Greatest Shots Journal:

1.

2.

3.

*David L. Cook*

Tournament site:

Date:

## Mental Toughness Journal:

Adversity     Negative Response     Mental Toughness Response

1.

2.

3.

*Psychology of Tournament Golf*

Tournament site:

Date:

## Greatest Shots Journal:

1.

2.

3.

*David L. Cook*

Tournament site:

Date:

## Mental Toughness Journal:

<u>Adversity</u>     <u>Negative Response</u>     <u>Mental Toughness Response</u>

1.

2.

3.

*Psychology of Tournament Golf*

Tournament site:

Date:

**Greatest Shots Journal:**

1.

2.

3.

*David L. Cook*

Tournament site:

Date:

## Mental Toughness Journal:

<u>Adversity</u>     <u>Negative Response</u>     <u>Mental Toughness Response</u>

1.

2.

3.

*Psychology of Tournament Golf*

Tournament site:

Date:

## Greatest Shots Journal:

1.

2.

3.

*David L. Cook*

Tournament site:

Date:

## Mental Toughness Journal:

| Adversity | Negative Response | Mental Toughness Response |

1.

2.

3.

*Psychology of Tournament Golf*

Tournament site:

Date:

## Greatest Shots Journal:

1.

2.

3.

*David L. Cook*

Tournament site:

Date:

## Mental Toughness Journal:

<u>Adversity</u>　　<u>Negative Response</u>　　<u>Mental Toughness Response</u>

1.

2.

3.

*Psychology of Tournament Golf*

Tournament site:

Date:

## Greatest Shots Journal:

1.

2.

3.

*David L. Cook*

Tournament site:

Date:

## Mental Toughness Journal:

<u>Adversity</u>    <u>Negative Response</u>    <u>Mental Toughness Response</u>

1.

2.

3.

*Psychology of Tournament Golf*

Tournament site:

Date:

### Greatest Shots Journal:

1.

2.

3.

*David L. Cook*

*Psychology of Tournament Golf*

*David L. Cook*